Contents

Introducing Division

12 creatures are divided into groups of 4.

There are 3 equal groups of 4.

12 ÷ 4 = 3

Did you know you can write division facts in two ways?	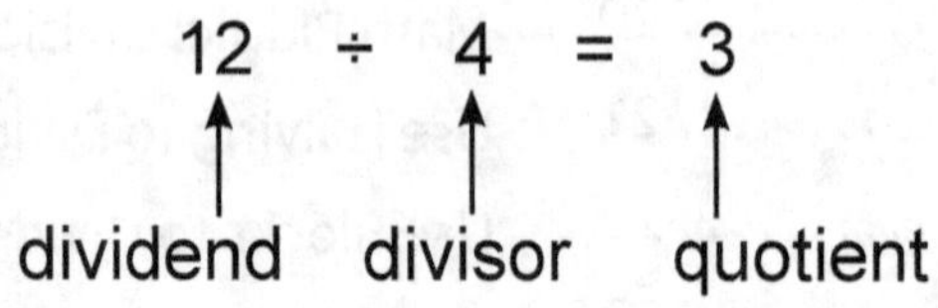	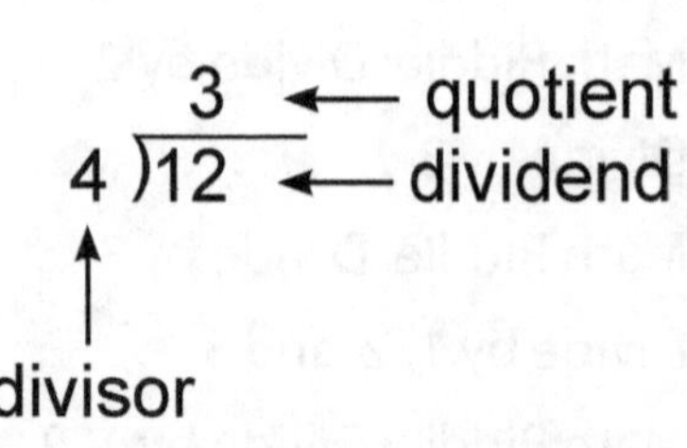

Write the division sentence.

_____ ÷ _____ = _____

_____ ÷ _____ = _____

_____ ÷ _____ = _____

Introducing Division

Write the division sentence.

_____ ÷ _____ = _____

_____)‾‾‾‾‾

_____ ÷ _____ = _____

_____)‾‾‾‾‾

_____ ÷ _____ = _____

_____)‾‾‾‾‾

_____ ÷ _____ = _____

_____)‾‾‾‾‾

_____ ÷ _____ = _____

_____)‾‾‾‾‾

Introducing Division

Write the division sentence.

___ ÷ ___ = ___

___ ÷ ___ = ___

___ ÷ ___ = ___

___ ÷ ___ = ___

___ ÷ ___ = ___

Introducing Division

Use a circle to divide into groups. Complete the division sentence.

Divide 10 creatures into groups of 5.

______ groups

$$10 \div 5 = \underline{\hspace{1cm}}$$

Divide 18 creatures into groups of 6.

______ groups

$$18 \div 6 = \underline{\hspace{1cm}}$$

Divide 8 creatures into groups of 2.

______ groups

$$8 \div 2 = \underline{\hspace{1cm}}$$

Divide 12 creatures into groups of 4.

______ groups

$$12 \div 4 = \underline{\hspace{1cm}}$$

Introducing Division

Use a circle to divide into groups. Complete the division sentence.

Divide 15 creatures into groups of 5.

______ groups   15 ÷ 5 = _______

Divide 9 creatures into groups of 3.

______ groups   9 ÷ 3 = _______

Divide 14 creatures into groups of 7.

______ groups   14 ÷ 7 = _______

Divide 16 creatures into groups of 4.

______ groups   16 ÷ 4 = _______

Divide by Skip Counting

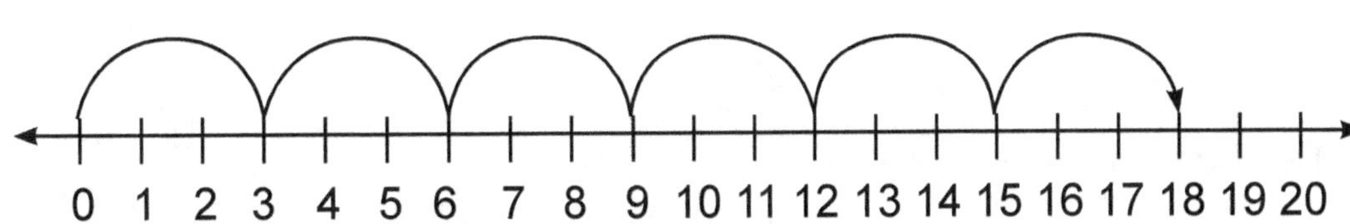

$18 \div 3 =$

It takes **6** skips of 3 to reach ___. $18 \div 3 = $ **6**

Skip count on the number line to divide. Write the answer.

$$= \underline{\hspace{2cm}}$$

$16 \div 4 =$

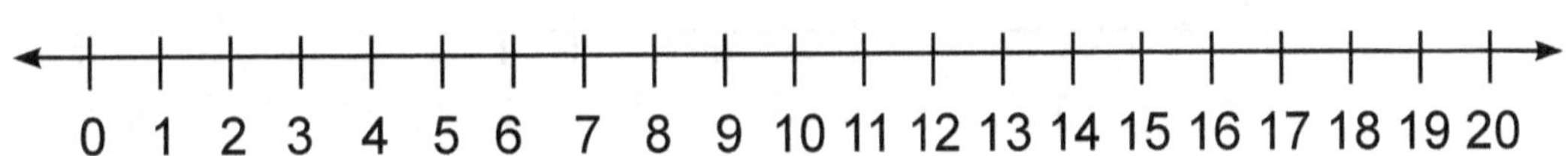

It takes ___ skips of 4 to reach ___. $16 \div 4 = $ ___

$$= \underline{\hspace{2cm}}$$

$15 \div 3 =$

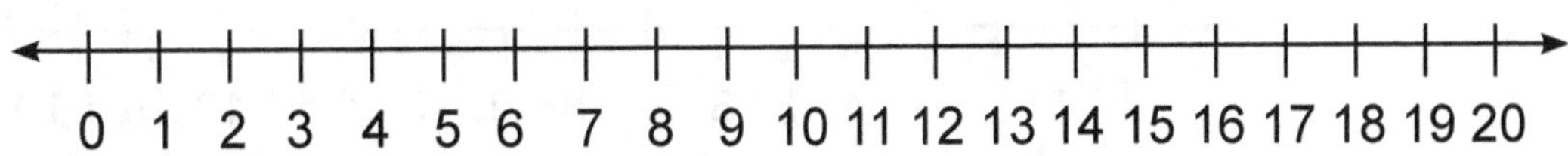

It takes ___ skips of ___ to reach ___. $15 \div 3 = $ ___

Divide by Skip Counting

Skip count on the number line to divide. Write the answer.

20 ÷ 5 =

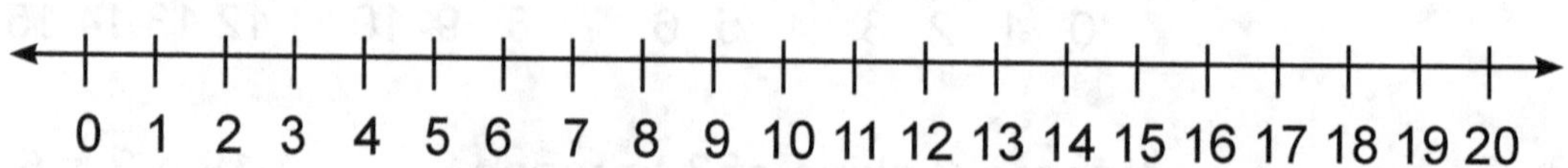

It takes ___ skips of ___ to reach ___.   20 ÷ 5 = ___

15 ÷ 5 =

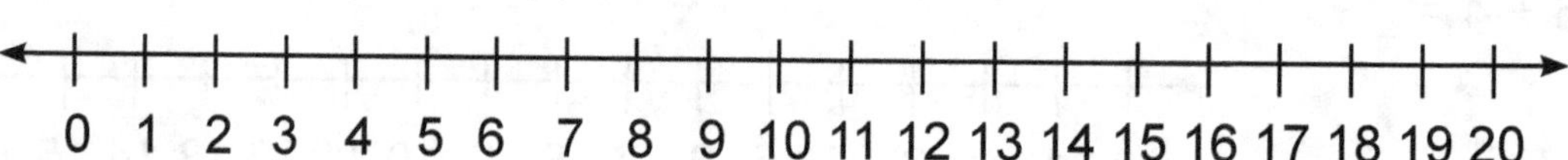

It takes ___ skips of ___ to reach ___.   15 ÷ 5 = ___

12 ÷ 4 =

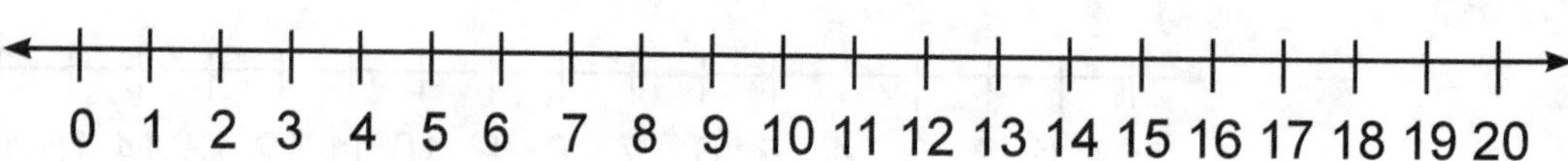

It takes ___ skips of ___ to reach ___.   12 ÷ 4 = ___

Divide by Skip Counting

Skip count on the number line to divide. Write the answer.

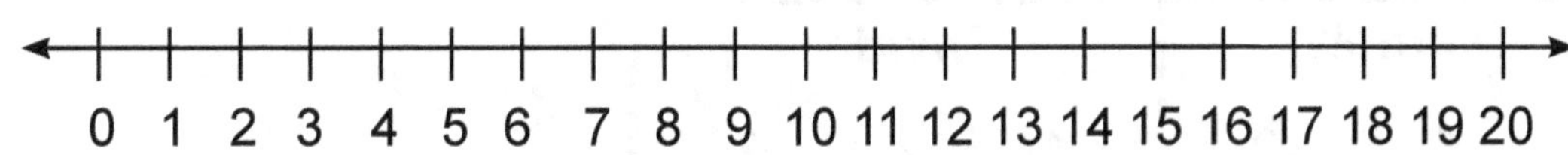

16 ÷ 2 =

It takes ___ skips of ___ to reach ___.   16 ÷ 2 = ___

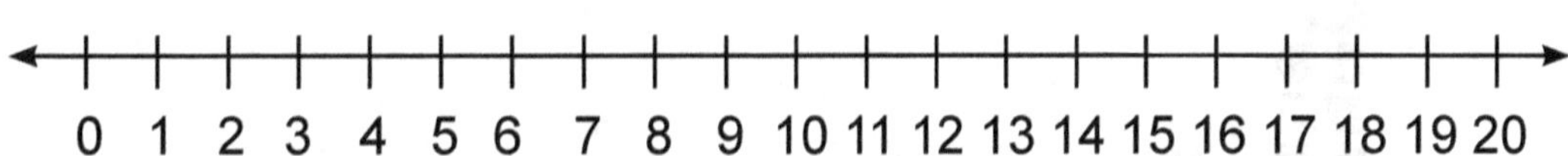

18 ÷ 3 =

It takes ___ skips of ___ to reach ___.   18 ÷ 3 = ___

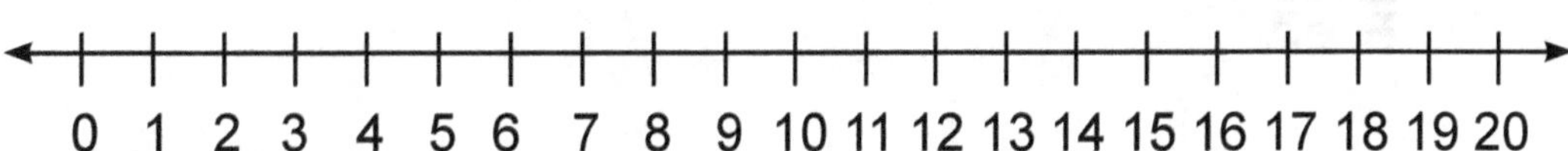

20 ÷ 4 =

It takes ___ skips of ___ to reach ___.   20 ÷ 4 = ___

Relate Multiplication to Division

Use the array to complete each number sentence.

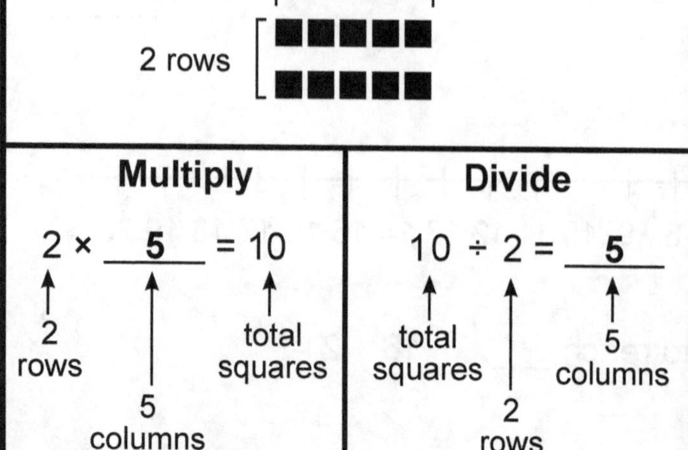

a)

3 × _______ = 15   15 ÷ 3 = _______

b)

_______ × 2 = 18   18 ÷ 9 = _______

c)

_______ × 4 = 16   16 ÷ 4 = _______

d)

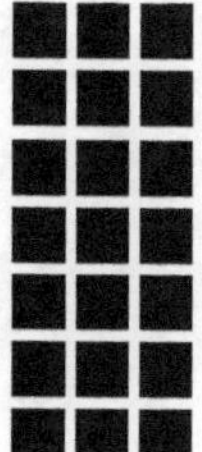

7 × _______ = 21   21 ÷ 7 = _______

e)

_______ × 10 = 40   40 ÷ 4 = _______

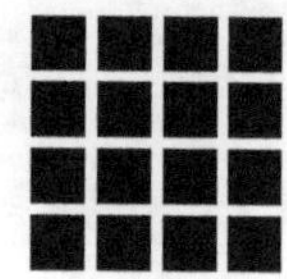

Relate Multiplication to Division

Use the array to complete each number sentence.

a) 

2 × _____ = 12

12 ÷ 2 = _____

b)

3 × _____ = 24

24 ÷ 3 = _____

c) 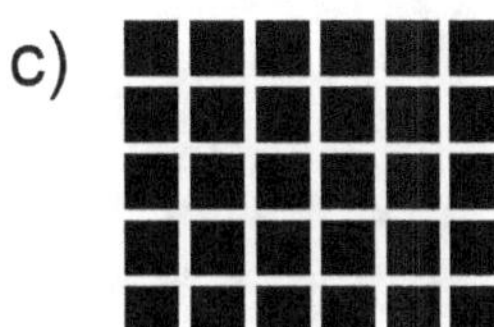

_____ × 6 = 30

30 ÷ 5 = _____

d) 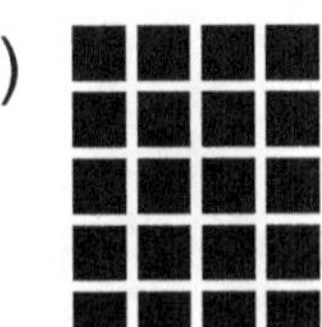

_____ × 4 = 20

20 ÷ 5 = _____

e) 

_____ × 9 = 27

27 ÷ 3 = _____

f)

_____ × 12 = 36

36 ÷ 3 = _____

Relate Multiplication to Division

Use the array to complete each number sentence.

a) 

$2 \times$ _____ $= 20$

$20 \div 2 =$ _____

b)

$3 \times$ _____ $= 33$

$33 \div 3 =$ _____

c) 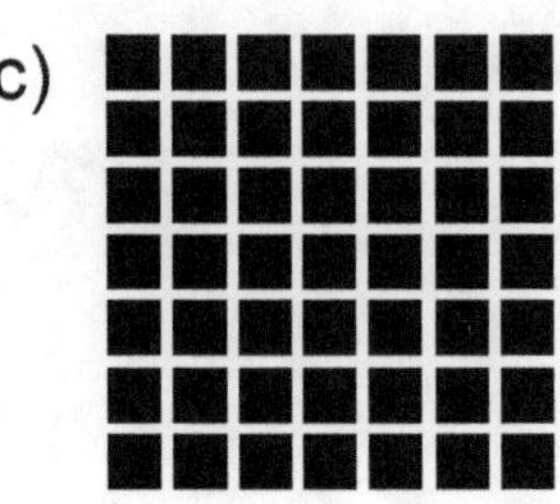

_____ $\times 7 = 49$

$49 \div 7 =$ _____

d)

_____ $\times 5 = 40$

$40 \div 8 =$ _____

e) 

$5 \times$ _____ $= 45$

$45 \div 5 =$ _____

f)

$5 \times$ _____ $= 60$

$60 \div 5 =$ _____

Use an Array to Find a Quotient

Draw an array to help you find each quotient.

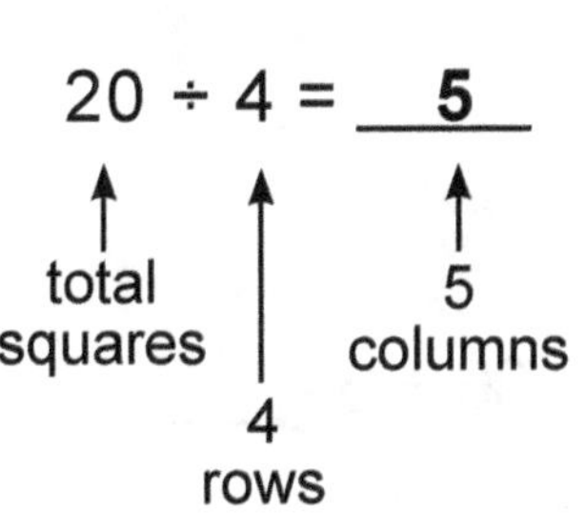

a)

$$15 \div 5 = \underline{\hspace{1cm}}$$

b)

$$14 \div 7 = \underline{\hspace{1cm}}$$

c)

$$20 \div 4 = \underline{\hspace{1cm}}$$

d)

$$12 \div 4 = \underline{\hspace{1cm}}$$

e)

$$8 \div 2 = \underline{\hspace{1cm}}$$

f)

$$9 \div 3 = \underline{\hspace{1cm}}$$

g)

$$16 \div 8 = \underline{\hspace{1cm}}$$

Use an Array to Find a Quotient

Draw an array to help you find each quotient.

a)

$25 \div 5 =$ _____

b)

$36 \div 6 =$ _____

c)

$60 \div 5 =$ _____

d)

$10 \div 2 =$ _____

e)

$24 \div 12 =$ _____

f)

$21 \div 3 =$ _____

g)

$40 \div 5 =$ _____

h)

$50 \div 5 =$ _____

Use an Array to Find a Quotient

Draw an array to help you find each quotient.

a)

$30 \div 5 = $ _____

b)

$24 \div 6 = $ _____

c)

$48 \div 12 = $ _____

d)

$32 \div 4 = $ _____

e)

$16 \div 2 = $ _____

f)

$27 \div 3 = $ _____

g)

$64 \div 8 = $ _____

h)

$70 \div 10 = $ _____

Relate Multiplication to Division

Use the multiplication fact to find each quotient.

a) $11 \times 3 = 33$

$33 \div 11 = \underline{\hspace{1cm}}$

b) $9 \times 7 = 63$

$63 \div 7 = \underline{\hspace{1cm}}$

c) $6 \times 7 = 42$

$42 \div 6 = \underline{\hspace{1cm}}$

d) $4 \times 10 = 40$

$40 \div 4 = \underline{\hspace{1cm}}$

e) $9 \times 5 = 45$

$45 \div 9 = \underline{\hspace{1cm}}$

f) $2 \times 8 = 16$

$16 \div 2 = \underline{\hspace{1cm}}$

g) $9 \times 9 = 81$

$81 \div 9 = \underline{\hspace{1cm}}$

h) $7 \times 11 = 77$

$77 \div 7 = \underline{\hspace{1cm}}$

i) $8 \times 1 = 8$

$8 \div 8 = \underline{\hspace{1cm}}$

j) $8 \times 5 = 40$

$40 \div 8 = \underline{\hspace{1cm}}$

k) $9 \times 12 = 108$

$108 \div 9 = \underline{\hspace{1cm}}$

l) $11 \times 11 = 121$

$121 \div 11 = \underline{\hspace{1cm}}$

Relate Multiplication to Division

Use the multiplication fact to find each quotient.

a) $2 \times 3 = 6$

$6 \div 2 = $ _____

b) $6 \times 9 = 54$

$54 \div 6 = $ _____

c) $2 \times 8 = 16$

$16 \div 2 = $ _____

d) $4 \times 7 = 28$

$28 \div 4 = $ _____

e) $7 \times 12 = 84$

$84 \div 7 = $ _____

f) $5 \times 6 = 30$

$30 \div 5 = $ _____

g) $9 \times 2 = 18$

$18 \div 9 = $ _____

h) $8 \times 11 = 88$

$88 \div 8 = $ _____

i) $9 \times 1 = 9$

$9 \div 9 = $ _____

j) $6 \times 8 = 48$

$48 \div 6 = $ _____

k) $9 \times 11 = 99$

$99 \div 9 = $ _____

l) $11 \times 10 = 110$

$110 \div 11 = $ _____

Use Related Multiplication Facts to Divide with 0 and 1

The quotient is always 1 when any number other than 0 is divided by itself.

For example, $5 \div 5 = 1$.

Think of a related multiplication fact.

$5 \times 1 = 5$, so $5 \div 5 = 1$

The quotient is always the same as the dividend when any number is divided by 1.

For example, $8 \div 1 = 8$.

Think of a related multiplication fact.

$8 \times 1 = 8$, so $8 \div 1 = 8$

The quotient is always 0 when 0 is divided by any number other than 0.

For example, $0 \div 3 = 0$.

Think of a related multiplication fact.

$3 \times 0 = 0$, so $0 \div 3 = 0$

You cannot divide any number by 0.

Divide.

$0 \div 7 =$ _____ $12 \div 12 =$ _____ $10 \div 1 =$ _____ $0 \div 6 =$ _____

$5 \div 1 =$ _____ $0 \div 4 =$ _____ $3 \div 3 =$ _____ $7 \div 7 =$ _____

$0 \div 1 =$ _____ $11 \div 1 =$ _____ $0 \div 8 =$ _____ $6 \div 1 =$ _____

$8 \div 8 =$ _____ $0 \div 9 =$ _____ $9 \div 1 =$ _____ $0 \div 2 =$ _____

Divide by 2

Draw a line from the division sentence to the correct quotient. Hint: Practice skip counting by 2s.

0 ÷ 2 = ___	4
2 ÷ 2 = ___	9
4 ÷ 2 = ___	6
6 ÷ 2 = ___	8
8 ÷ 2 = ___	11
10 ÷ 2 = ___	3
12 ÷ 2 = ___	12
14 ÷ 2 = ___	7
16 ÷ 2 = ___	1
18 ÷ 2 = ___	10
20 ÷ 2 = ___	0
22 ÷ 2 = ___	5
24 ÷ 2 = ___	2

Math Riddle: Divide by 2

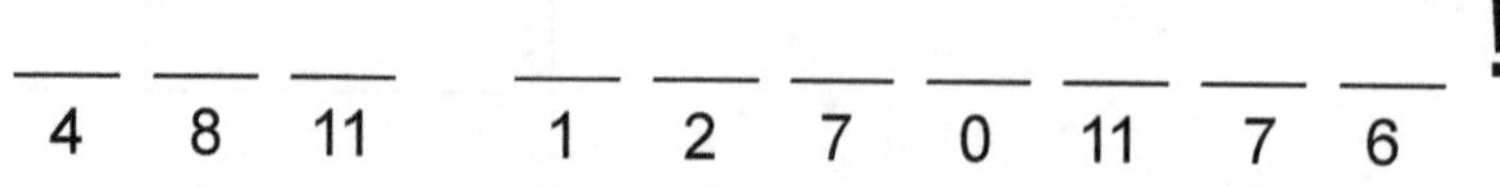

What is a polar bear's favorite food?

$$\overline{}\ \overline{}\ \overline{}\quad\overline{}\ \overline{}\ \overline{}\ \overline{}\ \overline{}\ \overline{}\ \overline{}\ !$$

  4   8 11   1 2 7 0 11 7 6

Watch out! Some letters are not used in the riddle!

Find the quotient.

A 18 ÷ 2 = ___	**B** 2 ÷ 2 = ___	**C** 16 ÷ 2 = ___
E 22 ÷ 2 = ___	**F** 6 ÷ 2 = ___	**G** 0 ÷ 2 = ___
I 8 ÷ 2 = ___	**M** 10 ÷ 2 = ___	**N** 24 ÷ 2 = ___
R 14 ÷ 2 = ___	**S** 12 ÷ 2 = ___	**U** 4 ÷ 2 = ___

Find the missing dividend.

___ ÷ 2 = 2	___ ÷ 2 = 8	___ ÷ 2 = 10	___ ÷ 2 = 1
___ ÷ 2 = 11	___ ÷ 2 = 6	___ ÷ 2 = 12	___ ÷ 2 = 0

Divide by 3

Draw a line from the division sentence to the correct quotient. Hint: Practice skip counting by 3s.

0 ÷ 3 = ___	6
3 ÷ 3 = ___	5
6 ÷ 3 = ___	9
9 ÷ 3 = ___	7
12 ÷ 3 = ___	10
15 ÷ 3 = ___	8
18 ÷ 3 = ___	11
21 ÷ 3 = ___	4
24 ÷ 3 = ___	12
27 ÷ 3 = ___	0
30 ÷ 3 = ___	1
33 ÷ 3 = ___	2
36 ÷ 3 = ___	3

Math Riddle: Divide by 3

What kind of hats do penguins wear?

$$\overline{}_{7}\ \overline{}_{8}\ \overline{}_{11}\quad \overline{}_{8}\ \overline{}_{5}\ \overline{}_{6}\ \overline{}_{4}\ !$$

Watch out! Some letters are not used in the riddle!

Find the quotient.

A	B	C
$15 \div 3 =$ ___	$3 \div 3 =$ ___	$24 \div 3 =$ ___
E $\quad 33 \div 3 =$ ___	**H** $\quad 6 \div 3 =$ ___	**I** $\quad 21 \div 3 =$ ___
M $\quad 27 \div 3 =$ ___	**N** $\quad 36 \div 3 =$ ___	**O** $\quad 30 \div 3 =$ ___
P $\quad 18 \div 3 =$ ___	**S** $\quad 12 \div 3 =$ ___	**T** $\quad 9 \div 3 =$ ___

Find the missing dividend.

___ $\div 3 = 6$	___ $\div 3 = 8$	___ $\div 3 = 5$	___ $\div 3 = 10$
___ $\div 3 = 7$	___ $\div 3 = 9$	___ $\div 3 = 12$	___ $\div 3 = 3$

Divide by 1, 2, and 3

Draw a line from the division sentence to the correct quotient. Color division facts with odd quotients red. Color the division facts with even quotients blue.

Left Column	Middle	Right Column
0 ÷ 1 =	3	9 ÷ 3 =
12 ÷ 2 =	9	5 ÷ 1 =
15 ÷ 3 =	7	21 ÷ 3 =
11 ÷ 1 =	5	24 ÷ 2 =
20 ÷ 2 =	10	1 ÷ 1 =
36 ÷ 3 =	4	22 ÷ 2 =
4 ÷ 2 =	12	12 ÷ 3 =
14 ÷ 2 =	2	10 ÷ 1 =
3 ÷ 3 =	6	16 ÷ 2 =
6 ÷ 2 =	11	18 ÷ 3 =
8 ÷ 2 =	1	27 ÷ 3 =
16 ÷ 2 =	0	4 ÷ 2 =
18 ÷ 2 =	8	0 ÷ 3 =

Divide by 1, 2, and 3

Find the quotient.

30 ÷ 3 = ___	10 ÷ 2 = ___	21 ÷ 3 = ___	1 ÷ 1 = ___
22 ÷ 2 = ___	36 ÷ 3 = ___	12 ÷ 1 = ___	8 ÷ 2 = ___
10 ÷ 1 = ___	24 ÷ 3 = ___	24 ÷ 2 = ___	8 ÷ 1 = ___
18 ÷ 3 = ___	6 ÷ 2 = ___	12 ÷ 3 = ___	11 ÷ 1 = ___
12 ÷ 2 = ___	7 ÷ 1 = ___	14 ÷ 2 = ___	33 ÷ 3 = ___
9 ÷ 3 = ___	5 ÷ 1 = ___	27 ÷ 3 = ___	0 ÷ 1 = ___
4 ÷ 2 = ___	6 ÷ 3 = ___	9 ÷ 1 = ___	2 ÷ 2 = ___

Divide by 1, 2, and 3

Find the quotient.

a) $1\overline{)6}$ b) $3\overline{)3}$ c) $2\overline{)12}$ d) $1\overline{)4}$

e) $3\overline{)24}$ f) $2\overline{)16}$ g) $2\overline{)8}$ h) $3\overline{)30}$

i) $2\overline{)4}$ j) $1\overline{)5}$ k) $3\overline{)12}$ l) $2\overline{)22}$

m) $2\overline{)18}$ n) $3\overline{)27}$ o) $1\overline{)8}$ p) $2\overline{)10}$

Math Riddle: Divide by 1, 2, and 3

Where do astronauts keep their lunch?

$$\overline{}\ \overline{}\quad \overline{}\quad \overline{}\ \overline{}\ \overline{}\ \overline{}\ \overline{}\ \overline{}\quad \overline{}\ \overline{}\ \overline{}\ !$$

7 10   8   4 8 9 10 12 3   11 5 1

Watch out! Some letters are not used in the riddle!

Find the quotient.

A	B	C	D
$3\overline{)24}$	$3\overline{)33}$	$3\overline{)36}$	$2\overline{)28}$
E	**F**	**G**	**H**
$3\overline{)6}$	$1\overline{)6}$	$2\overline{)4}$	$3\overline{)9}$
I	**J**	**K**	**L**
$2\overline{)14}$	$2\overline{)30}$	$1\overline{)2}$	$3\overline{)12}$
M	**N**	**O**	**R**
$2\overline{)12}$	$3\overline{)30}$	$2\overline{)10}$	$3\overline{)18}$
S	**U**	**V**	**X**
$3\overline{)6}$	$3\overline{)27}$	$3\overline{)15}$	$1\overline{)1}$

Divide by 4

Draw a line from the division sentence to the correct quotient. Hint: Practice skip counting by 4s.

$0 \div 4 = \underline{}$	9
$4 \div 4 = \underline{}$	4
$8 \div 4 = \underline{}$	6
$12 \div 4 = \underline{}$	0
$16 \div 4 = \underline{}$	1
$20 \div 4 = \underline{}$	12
$24 \div 4 = \underline{}$	3
$28 \div 4 = \underline{}$	7
$32 \div 4 = \underline{}$	10
$36 \div 4 = \underline{}$	11
$40 \div 4 = \underline{}$	8
$44 \div 4 = \underline{}$	5
$48 \div 4 = \underline{}$	2

Math Riddle: Divide by 4

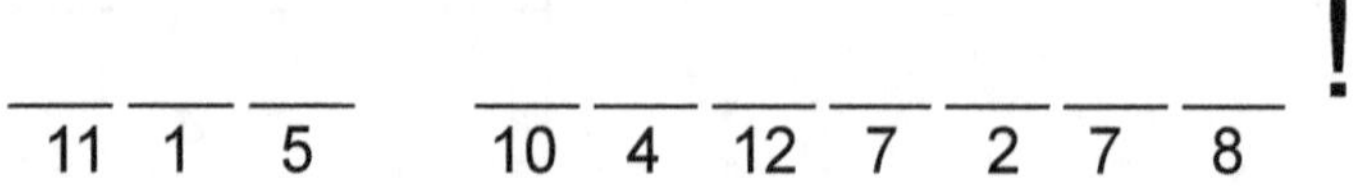

__ __ __ __ __ __ __ __ __ __ !
11 1 5   10 4 12 7 2 7 8

Watch out! Some letters are not used in the riddle!

Find the quotient.

A	B	E
8 ÷ 4 = ___	48 ÷ 4 = ___	20 ÷ 4 = ___
H	**I**	**L**
4 ÷ 4 = ___	16 ÷ 4 = ___	40 ÷ 4 = ___
M	**N**	**R**
36 ÷ 4 = ___	12 ÷ 4 = ___	28 ÷ 4 = ___
S	**T**	**Y**
24 ÷ 4 = ___	44 ÷ 4 = ___	32 ÷ 4 = ___

Find the missing dividend.

___ ÷ 4 = 2	___ ÷ 4 = 9	___ ÷ 4 = 3	___ ÷ 4 = 1
___ ÷ 4 = 10	___ ÷ 4 = 7	___ ÷ 4 = 12	___ ÷ 4 = 5

Divide by 5

Draw a line from the division sentence to the correct quotient. Hint: Practice skip counting by 5s.

0 ÷ 5 = ___	4
5 ÷ 5 = ___	9
10 ÷ 5 = ___	8
15 ÷ 5 = ___	5
20 ÷ 5 = ___	10
25 ÷ 5 = ___	3
30 ÷ 5 = ___	12
35 ÷ 5 = ___	1
40 ÷ 5 = ___	7
45 ÷ 5 = ___	11
50 ÷ 5 = ___	2
55 ÷ 5 = ___	6
60 ÷ 5 = ___	0

Math Riddle: Divide by 5

What belongs to you but is used more by other people?

$$\overline{}\ \overline{}\ \overline{}\ \overline{}\quad \overline{}\ \overline{}\ \overline{}\ \overline{}\ !$$

6 12 10 4   1 2 7 5

Watch out! Some letters are not used in the riddle!

Find the quotient.

A 10 ÷ 5 = ___	**C** 40 ÷ 5 = ___	**E** 25 ÷ 5 = ___
G 45 ÷ 5 = ___	**M** 35 ÷ 5 = ___	**N** 5 ÷ 5 = ___
O 60 ÷ 5 = ___	**R** 20 ÷ 5 = ___	**S** 55 ÷ 5 = ___
U 50 ÷ 5 = ___	**W** 15 ÷ 5 = ___	**Y** 30 ÷ 5 = ___

Find the missing dividend.

___ ÷ 5 = 8	___ ÷ 5 = 12	___ ÷ 5 = 10	___ ÷ 5 = 6
___ ÷ 5 = 3	___ ÷ 5 = 7	___ ÷ 5 = 9	___ ÷ 5 = 1

Divide by 6

Draw a line from the division sentence to the correct quotient. Hint: Practice skip counting by 6s.

Division sentence		Quotient
0 ÷ 6 = ___		8
6 ÷ 6 = ___		9
12 ÷ 6 = ___		6
18 ÷ 6 = ___		5
24 ÷ 6 = ___		11
30 ÷ 6 = ___		7
36 ÷ 6 = ___		12
42 ÷ 6 = ___		3
48 ÷ 6 = ___		10
54 ÷ 6 = ___		4
60 ÷ 6 = ___		0
66 ÷ 6 = ___		1
72 ÷ 6 = ___		2

Math Riddle: Divide by 6

What did the tornado say to the sports car?

$$\overline{\quad}\,,\ \overline{7}\ \overline{8}\ \overline{10}\ \overline{11}\quad \overline{6}\ \overline{9}\quad \overline{12}\ \overline{9}\ \overline{4}\quad \overline{3}\quad \overline{11}\ \overline{5}\ \overline{2}\ \overline{1}\ !$$

Find the quotient.

A	E	F
18 ÷ 6 = ___	48 ÷ 6 = ___	72 ÷ 6 = ___
G	**I**	**L**
36 ÷ 6 = ___	12 ÷ 6 = ___	42 ÷ 6 = ___
N	**O**	**P**
6 ÷ 6 = ___	54 ÷ 6 = ___	30 ÷ 6 = ___
R	**S**	**T**
24 ÷ 6 = ___	66 ÷ 6 = ___	60 ÷ 6 = ___

Find the missing dividend.

___ ÷ 6 = 10	___ ÷ 6 = 8	___ ÷ 6 = 11	___ ÷ 6 = 5
___ ÷ 6 = 9	___ ÷ 6 = 4	___ ÷ 6 = 7	___ ÷ 6 = 3

Divide by 4, 5, and 6

Draw a line from the division sentence to the correct quotient. Color division facts with odd quotients red. Color the division facts with even quotients blue.

Column 1	Middle	Column 3
$0 \div 6 =$	7	$10 \div 5 =$
$60 \div 5 =$	9	$28 \div 4 =$
$8 \div 4 =$	4	$20 \div 4 =$
$66 \div 6 =$	5	$0 \div 5 =$
$20 \div 5 =$	12	$32 \div 4 =$
$36 \div 6 =$	3	$24 \div 6 =$
$6 \div 6 =$	10	$50 \div 5 =$
$35 \div 5 =$	2	$44 \div 4 =$
$12 \div 4 =$	0	$48 \div 4 =$
$54 \div 6 =$	8	$45 \div 5 =$
$40 \div 5 =$	1	$6 \div 6 =$
$40 \div 4 =$	6	$24 \div 4 =$
$30 \div 6 =$	11	$15 \div 5 =$

Divide by 4, 5, and 6

Find the quotient.

32 ÷ 4 = ___	5 ÷ 5 = ___	66 ÷ 6 = ___	36 ÷ 4 = ___
25 ÷ 5 = ___	36 ÷ 6 = ___	4 ÷ 4 = ___	0 ÷ 5 = ___
12 ÷ 6 = ___	24 ÷ 4 = ___	35 ÷ 5 = ___	6 ÷ 6 = ___
16 ÷ 4 = ___	45 ÷ 5 = ___	54 ÷ 6 = ___	12 ÷ 4 = ___
10 ÷ 5 = ___	18 ÷ 6 = ___	28 ÷ 4 = ___	15 ÷ 5 = ___
24 ÷ 6 = ___	48 ÷ 4 = ___	50 ÷ 5 = ___	72 ÷ 6 = ___
0 ÷ 4 = ___	20 ÷ 5 = ___	48 ÷ 6 = ___	8 ÷ 4 = ___

Divide by 4, 5, and 6

Find the quotient.

a) $4\overline{)24}$	b) $5\overline{)5}$	c) $6\overline{)18}$	d) $4\overline{)44}$
e) $6\overline{)60}$	f) $4\overline{)20}$	g) $5\overline{)10}$	h) $6\overline{)30}$
i) $5\overline{)35}$	j) $6\overline{)42}$	k) $4\overline{)4}$	l) $5\overline{)55}$
m) $4\overline{)28}$	n) $5\overline{)20}$	o) $6\overline{)66}$	p) $4\overline{)12}$

Math Riddle: Divide by 4, 5, and 6

When does the Moon weigh the most?

$$\overline{}\ \overline{}\ \overline{}\ \overline{}\quad \overline{}\ \overline{}\quad \overline{}\ \overline{}\quad \overline{}\ \overline{}\ \overline{}\ \overline{}\ !$$

9 4 1 3   11 8   11 2   5 10 7 7

Watch out! Some letters are not used in the riddle!

Find the quotient.

E	F	G	H
$6\overline{)6}$	$5\overline{)25}$	$6\overline{)72}$	$5\overline{)20}$
I $\;4\overline{)44}$	**K** $\;5\overline{)30}$	**L** $\;5\overline{)35}$	**M** $\;5\overline{)0}$
N $\;4\overline{)12}$	**O** $\;4\overline{)24}$	**P** $\;4\overline{)48}$	**S** $\;5\overline{)10}$
T $\;6\overline{)48}$	**U** $\;5\overline{)50}$	**W** $\;5\overline{)45}$	**X** $\;6\overline{)36}$

Divide by 7

Draw a line from the division sentence to the correct quotient. Hint: Practice skip counting by 7s.

0 ÷ 7 = ___	8
7 ÷ 7 = ___	6
14 ÷ 7 = ___	9
21 ÷ 7 = ___	1
28 ÷ 7 = ___	3
35 ÷ 7 = ___	11
42 ÷ 7 = ___	4
49 ÷ 7 = ___	7
56 ÷ 7 = ___	12
63 ÷ 7 = ___	2
70 ÷ 7 = ___	0
77 ÷ 7 = ___	5
84 ÷ 7 = ___	10

Math Riddle: Divide by 7

How did the robot make the number seven even?

Watch out! Some letters are not used in the riddle!

<u>   </u> <u>   </u> <u>   </u> <u>   </u> <u>   </u> <u>   </u> <u>   </u> <u>   </u> <u>   </u> <u>   </u> <u>   </u> <u>   </u> <u>   </u> <u>   </u>!

11 9 7   10 5 5 6   5 4 10   10 9 7 11

Find the quotient.

A $14 \div 7 =$ ___	**C** $84 \div 7 =$ ___	**D** $21 \div 7 =$ ___
E $49 \div 7 =$ ___	**H** $63 \div 7 =$ ___	**K** $42 \div 7 =$ ___
O $35 \div 7 =$ ___	**P** $56 \div 7 =$ ___	**S** $77 \div 7 =$ ___
T $70 \div 7 =$ ___	**U** $28 \div 7 =$ ___	**W** $7 \div 7 =$ ___

Find the missing dividend.

___ $\div 7 = 5$	___ $\div 7 = 8$	___ $\div 7 = 12$	___ $\div 7 = 4$
___ $\div 7 = 10$	___ $\div 7 = 2$	___ $\div 7 = 6$	___ $\div 7 = 3$

Divide by 8

Draw a line from the division sentence to the correct quotient. Hint: Practice skip counting by 8s.

Division sentences		Quotients
$0 \div 8 = \underline{\quad}$		4
$8 \div 8 = \underline{\quad}$		9
$16 \div 8 = \underline{\quad}$		6
$24 \div 8 = \underline{\quad}$		8
$32 \div 8 = \underline{\quad}$		11
$40 \div 8 = \underline{\quad}$		3
$48 \div 8 = \underline{\quad}$		12
$56 \div 8 = \underline{\quad}$		7
$64 \div 8 = \underline{\quad}$		1
$72 \div 8 = \underline{\quad}$		10
$80 \div 8 = \underline{\quad}$		0
$88 \div 8 = \underline{\quad}$		5
$96 \div 8 = \underline{\quad}$		2

Math Riddle: Divide by 8

What has four legs but cannot walk?

___ ___ ___ ___ ___ ___ !
 3   9   2   3   5   8

Watch out! Some letters are not used in the riddle!

Find the quotient.

A	B	C
$24 \div 8 = $ ___	$48 \div 8 = $ ___	$72 \div 8 = $ ___
E	**H**	**I**
$32 \div 8 = $ ___	$16 \div 8 = $ ___	$40 \div 8 = $ ___
J	**K**	**L**
$96 \div 8 = $ ___	$56 \div 8 = $ ___	$80 \div 8 = $ ___
P	**Q**	**R**
$88 \div 8 = $ ___	$8 \div 8 = $ ___	$64 \div 8 = $ ___

Find the missing dividend.

___ $\div 8 = 2$	___ $\div 8 = 11$	___ $\div 8 = 8$	___ $\div 8 = 4$
___ $\div 8 = 10$	___ $\div 8 = 3$	___ $\div 8 = 9$	___ $\div 8 = 12$

Divide by 9

Draw a line from the division sentence to the correct quotient. Hint: Practice skip counting by 9s.

Division Sentence		Quotient
0 ÷ 9 = ___		7
9 ÷ 9 = ___		9
18 ÷ 9 = ___		2
27 ÷ 9 = ___		8
36 ÷ 9 = ___		4
45 ÷ 9 = ___		12
54 ÷ 9 = ___		3
63 ÷ 9 = ___		11
72 ÷ 9 = ___		6
81 ÷ 9 = ___		5
90 ÷ 9 = ___		0
99 ÷ 9 = ___		10
108 ÷ 9 = ___		1

Math Riddle: Divide by 9

Where do fish like to sleep?

$$\overline{}\ \overline{}\ \overline{}\quad \overline{}\ \overline{}\ \overline{}\ \overline{}\ \overline{}\ \overline{}\ !$$
6   10   4   1   2   4   5   2   9

Watch out! Some letters are not used in the riddle!

Find the quotient.

A	B	C
36 ÷ 9 = ___	45 ÷ 9 = ___	72 ÷ 9 = ___
D 81 ÷ 9 = ___	**E** 18 ÷ 9 = ___	**M** 99 ÷ 9 = ___
N 90 ÷ 9 = ___	**O** 54 ÷ 9 = ___	**P** 27 ÷ 9 = ___
R 108 ÷ 9 = ___	**S** 9 ÷ 9 = ___	**T** 63 ÷ 9 = ___

Find the missing dividend.

___ ÷ 9 = 10	___ ÷ 9 = 8	___ ÷ 9 = 11	___ ÷ 9 = 5
___ ÷ 9 = 9	___ ÷ 9 = 4	___ ÷ 9 = 7	___ ÷ 9 = 3

Divide by 7, 8, and 9

Draw a line from the division sentence to the correct quotient. Color division facts with odd quotients red. Color the division facts with even quotients blue.

$0 \div 9 =$	**11**	$63 \div 7 =$
$64 \div 8 =$	**5**	$28 \div 7 =$
$77 \div 7 =$	**4**	$0 \div 8 =$
$108 \div 9 =$	**9**	$27 \div 9 =$
$40 \div 8 =$	**12**	$72 \div 9 =$
$70 \div 7 =$	**2**	$42 \div 7 =$
$63 \div 9 =$	**1**	$7 \div 7 =$
$8 \div 8 =$	**3**	$45 \div 9 =$
$21 \div 7 =$	**6**	$16 \div 8 =$
$54 \div 9 =$	**8**	$49 \div 7 =$
$32 \div 8 =$	**10**	$96 \div 8 =$
$14 \div 7 =$	**0**	$88 \div 8 =$
$81 \div 9 =$	**7**	$90 \div 9 =$

Divide by 7, 8, and 9

Find the quotient.

$35 \div 7 = $ ___	$8 \div 8 = $ ___	$108 \div 9 = $ ___	$70 \div 7 = $ ___
$24 \div 8 = $ ___	$45 \div 9 = $ ___	$21 \div 7 = $ ___	$0 \div 8 = $ ___
$9 \div 9 = $ ___	$56 \div 7 = $ ___	$32 \div 8 = $ ___	$81 \div 9 = $ ___
$14 \div 7 = $ ___	$64 \div 8 = $ ___	$54 \div 9 = $ ___	$0 \div 7 = $ ___
$16 \div 8 = $ ___	$90 \div 9 = $ ___	$28 \div 7 = $ ___	$48 \div 8 = $ ___
$63 \div 9 = $ ___	$42 \div 7 = $ ___	$56 \div 8 = $ ___	$72 \div 9 = $ ___
$49 \div 7 = $ ___	$80 \div 8 = $ ___	$99 \div 9 = $ ___	$84 \div 7 = $ ___

Divide by 7, 8, and 9

Find the quotient.

a) $7\overline{)49}$ b) $8\overline{)96}$ c) $8\overline{)24}$ d) $9\overline{)18}$

e) $8\overline{)64}$ f) $9\overline{)99}$ g) $7\overline{)56}$ h) $8\overline{)40}$

i) $7\overline{)63}$ j) $8\overline{)56}$ k) $9\overline{)90}$ l) $7\overline{)70}$

m) $9\overline{)54}$ n) $7\overline{)42}$ o) $8\overline{)48}$ p) $9\overline{)27}$

Math Riddle: Divide by 7, 8, and 9

Where do astronauts go to see the stars?

$\overline{}\ \overline{}\ \overline{}\ \overline{}\ \overline{}\ \overline{}\ \overline{}\ \overline{}\ \overline{}$!

10 7 1 1 3 11 7 7 8

Watch out! Some letters are not used in the riddle!

Find the quotient.

A $7\overline{)28}$	B $8\overline{)72}$	C $9\overline{)45}$	D $7\overline{)56}$
E $7\overline{)42}$	F $9\overline{)18}$	G $7\overline{)14}$	H $8\overline{)80}$
I $8\overline{)48}$	N $8\overline{)32}$	K $9\overline{)108}$	L $7\overline{)7}$
M $9\overline{)54}$	O $9\overline{)63}$	P $7\overline{)35}$	R $8\overline{)96}$
S $7\overline{)84}$	U $8\overline{)40}$	W $8\overline{)88}$	Y $7\overline{)21}$

Divide by 10

Draw a line from the division sentence to the correct quotient. Hint: Practice skip counting by 10s.

0 ÷ 10 = ___	3
10 ÷ 10 = ___	4
20 ÷ 10 = ___	10
30 ÷ 10 = ___	6
40 ÷ 10 = ___	11
50 ÷ 10 = ___	9
60 ÷ 10 = ___	7
70 ÷ 10 = ___	1
80 ÷ 10 = ___	12
90 ÷ 10 = ___	0
100 ÷ 10 = ___	8
110 ÷ 10 = ___	2
120 ÷ 10 = ___	5

Math Riddle: Divide by 10

What do you call a famous fish?

__ __ __ __ __ __ __ __ __ !
8   7   5   8   3   9   6   7   2

Watch out! Some letters are not used in the riddle!

Find the quotient.

A	B	E
80 ÷ 10 = ___	40 ÷ 10 = ___	120 ÷ 10 = ___
F	**G**	**H**
90 ÷ 10 = ___	110 ÷ 10 = ___	20 ÷ 10 = ___
I	**J**	**R**
60 ÷ 10 = ___	100 ÷ 10 = ___	30 ÷ 10 = ___
S	**T**	**Y**
70 ÷ 10 = ___	50 ÷ 10 = ___	10 ÷ 10 = ___

Find the missing dividend.

___ ÷ 10 = 3	___ ÷ 10 = 8	___ ÷ 10 = 12	___ ÷ 10 = 6
___ ÷ 10 = 11	___ ÷ 10 = 5	___ ÷ 10 = 7	___ ÷ 10 = 9

Divide by 11

Draw a line from the division sentence to the correct quotient. Hint: Practice skip counting by 11s.

Division Sentences		Quotients
$0 \div 11 = \underline{\quad}$		11
$11 \div 11 = \underline{\quad}$		0
$22 \div 11 = \underline{\quad}$		6
$33 \div 11 = \underline{\quad}$		8
$44 \div 11 = \underline{\quad}$		9
$55 \div 11 = \underline{\quad}$		3
$66 \div 11 = \underline{\quad}$		4
$77 \div 11 = \underline{\quad}$		2
$88 \div 11 = \underline{\quad}$		12
$99 \div 11 = \underline{\quad}$		5
$110 \div 11 = \underline{\quad}$		10
$121 \div 11 = \underline{\quad}$		1
$132 \div 11 = \underline{\quad}$		7

Math Riddle: Divide by 11

What animal is smarter than a talking dinosaur?

___   ___ ___ ___ ___ ___ ___ ___ ___   ___ ___ ___ !
3   6   2   4   1   1   10   12   7   11   4   4

Watch out! Some letters are not used in the riddle!

Find the quotient.

A 33 ÷ 11 = ___	**B** 121 ÷ 11 = ___	**C** 55 ÷ 11 = ___
E 44 ÷ 11 = ___	**G** 77 ÷ 11 = ___	**I** 110 ÷ 11 = ___
J 99 ÷ 11 = ___	**L** 11 ÷ 11 = ___	**N** 132 ÷ 11 = ___
P 22 ÷ 11 = ___	**S** 66 ÷ 11 = ___	**T** 88 ÷ 11 = ___

Find the missing dividend.

___ ÷ 11 = 3	___ ÷ 11 = 4	___ ÷ 11 = 8	___ ÷ 11 = 12
___ ÷ 11 = 9	___ ÷ 11 = 10	___ ÷ 11 = 5	___ ÷ 11 = 2

Divide by 12

Draw a line from the division sentence to the correct quotient. Hint: Practice skip counting by 12s.

$0 \div 12 =$ ___	10
$12 \div 12 =$ ___	8
$24 \div 12 =$ ___	6
$36 \div 12 =$ ___	12
$48 \div 12 =$ ___	5
$60 \div 12 =$ ___	9
$72 \div 12 =$ ___	11
$84 \div 12 =$ ___	0
$96 \div 12 =$ ___	2
$108 \div 12 =$ ___	4
$120 \div 12 =$ ___	1
$132 \div 12 =$ ___	7
$144 \div 12 =$ ___	3

Math Riddle: Divide by 12

What did the dog say to the flea?

__ __ __ __   __ __ __ __ __ __ __   __ __ !
10 9 11 7   4   5   8   8   1   2   8   12   6

Find the quotient.

A	B	E
36 ÷ 12 = ___	48 ÷ 12 = ___	72 ÷ 12 = ___
I 12 ÷ 12 = ___	**G** 96 ÷ 12 = ___	**M** 144 ÷ 12 = ___
N 24 ÷ 12 = ___	**O** 132 ÷ 12 = ___	**P** 84 ÷ 12 = ___
S 120 ÷ 12 = ___	**T** 108 ÷ 12 = ___	**U** 60 ÷ 12 = ___

Find the missing dividend.

___ ÷ 12 = 11	___ ÷ 12 = 2	___ ÷ 12 = 9	___ ÷ 12 = 6
___ ÷ 12 = 5	___ ÷ 12 = 8	___ ÷ 12 = 7	___ ÷ 12 = 4

Divide by 10, 11, and 12

Draw a line from the division sentence to the correct quotient. Color division facts with odd quotients red. Color the division facts with even quotients blue.

Left column	Center	Right column
121 ÷ 11 =	7	40 ÷ 10 =
60 ÷ 12 =	9	72 ÷ 12 =
80 ÷ 10 =	4	22 ÷ 11 =
99 ÷ 11 =	5	10 ÷ 10 =
24 ÷ 12 =	12	36 ÷ 12 =
100 ÷ 10 =	3	121 ÷ 11 =
11 ÷ 11 =	10	110 ÷ 11 =
0 ÷ 12 =	2	108 ÷ 12 =
60 ÷ 10 =	0	55 ÷ 11 =
132 ÷ 11 =	8	84 ÷ 12 =
48 ÷ 12 =	1	0 ÷ 10 =
30 ÷ 10 =	6	88 ÷ 11 =
77 ÷ 11 =	11	144 ÷ 12 =

Divide by 10, 11, and 12

Find the quotient.

30 ÷ 10 = ___	110 ÷ 11 = ___	108 ÷ 12 = ___	50 ÷ 10 = ___
55 ÷ 11 = ___	36 ÷ 12 = ___	90 ÷ 10 = ___	0 ÷ 11 = ___
144 ÷ 12 = ___	80 ÷ 10 = ___	22 ÷ 11 = ___	48 ÷ 12 = ___
100 ÷ 10 = ___	44 ÷ 11 = ___	84 ÷ 12 = ___	120 ÷ 10 = ___
33 ÷ 11 = ___	60 ÷ 12 = ___	20 ÷ 10 = ___	88 ÷ 11 = ___
24 ÷ 12 = ___	70 ÷ 10 = ___	11 ÷ 11 = ___	72 ÷ 12 = ___
40 ÷ 10 = ___	66 ÷ 11 = ___	96 ÷ 12 = ___	10 ÷ 10 = ___

Divide by 10, 11, and 12

Find the quotient.

a) $10\overline{)60}$ b) $11\overline{)33}$ c) $12\overline{)12}$ d) $10\overline{)40}$

e) $12\overline{)24}$ f) $10\overline{)70}$ g) $11\overline{)55}$ h) $12\overline{)60}$

i) $11\overline{)44}$ j) $12\overline{)144}$ k) $10\overline{)120}$ l) $11\overline{)22}$

m) $10\overline{)90}$ n) $11\overline{)77}$ o) $12\overline{)36}$ p) $10\overline{)10}$

Math Riddle: Divide by 10, 11, and 12

How do astronauts organize a trip to outer space?

$$\overline{}_{3}\ \overline{}_{10}\ \overline{}_{7}\ \overline{}_{12}\qquad \overline{}_{5}\ \overline{}_{9}\ \overline{}_{11}\ \overline{}_{8}\ \overline{}_{7}\ \overline{}_{3}\ !$$

Watch out! Some letters are not used in the riddle!

Find the quotient.

A	B	C	D
11)121	12)12	12)48	11)22
E	**F**	**G**	**H**
11)77	11)11	10)40	12)120
I	**K**	**L**	**M**
12)72	11)66	12)108	10)10
N	**O**	**P**	**R**
12)96	10)60	10)50	11)44
S	**T**	**V**	**Y**
10)20	12)36	12)0	11)132

Division Facts from 0 to 12

Draw a line from the division sentence to the correct quotient. Color division facts with odd quotients red. Color the division facts with even quotients blue.

Column 1	Center	Column 3
$7 \div 1 =$ _____	**12**	$12 \div 2 =$ _____
$22 \div 2 =$ _____	**5**	$20 \div 5 =$ _____
$6 \div 2 =$ _____	**8**	$48 \div 6 =$ _____
$72 \div 12 =$ _____	**10**	$24 \div 8 =$ _____
$45 \div 5 =$ _____	**3**	$0 \div 8 =$ _____
$12 \div 6 =$ _____	**7**	$84 \div 12 =$ _____
$70 \div 7 =$ _____	**4**	$3 \div 3 =$ _____
$16 \div 4 =$ _____	**2**	$25 \div 5 =$ _____
$108 \div 9 =$ _____	**0**	$132 \div 11 =$ _____
$10 \div 10 =$ _____	**11**	$81 \div 9 =$ _____
$55 \div 11 =$ _____	**9**	$24 \div 12 =$ _____
$0 \div 12 =$ _____	**1**	$121 \div 11 =$ _____
$32 \div 4 =$ _____	**6**	$100 \div 10 =$ _____

Missing Dividends: Division Facts

Fill in the missing dividend.

___ ÷ 2 = 2   ___ ÷ 10 = 8   ___ ÷ 9 = 10   ___ ÷ 4 = 1

___ ÷ 5 = 10   ___ ÷ 6 = 6   ___ ÷ 3 = 6   ___ ÷ 12 = 5

___ ÷ 8 = 11   ___ ÷ 12 = 12   ___ ÷ 11 = 5   ___ ÷ 5 = 0

___ ÷ 7 = 12   ___ ÷ 9 = 2   ___ ÷ 7 = 10   ___ ÷ 5 = 9

___ ÷ 11 = 4   ___ ÷ 2 = 7   ___ ÷ 3 = 12   ___ ÷ 4 = 7

___ ÷ 3 = 3   ___ ÷ 6 = 9   ___ ÷ 10 = 2   ___ ÷ 1 = 3

___ ÷ 9 = 11   ___ ÷ 4 = 10   ___ ÷ 6 = 7   ___ ÷ 12 = 4

Missing Dividends: Division Facts

Fill in the missing dividend.

___ ÷ 9 = 2	___ ÷ 5 = 8	___ ÷ 6 = 10	___ ÷ 1 = 1
___ ÷ 7 = 10	___ ÷ 8 = 6	___ ÷ 4 = 6	___ ÷ 4 = 4
___ ÷ 3 = 11	___ ÷ 11 = 12	___ ÷ 9 = 5	___ ÷ 10 = 0
___ ÷ 9 = 12	___ ÷ 8 = 2	___ ÷ 12 = 10	___ ÷ 4 = 9
___ ÷ 10 = 4	___ ÷ 11 = 7	___ ÷ 11 = 8	___ ÷ 5 = 7
___ ÷ 6 = 3	___ ÷ 1 = 9	___ ÷ 1 = 2	___ ÷ 12 = 3
___ ÷ 4 = 11	___ ÷ 2 = 10	___ ÷ 8 = 7	___ ÷ 1 = 4

Math Riddle: Division Fun

I am a robot shaped like a human being. What am I?

___ ___ ___ ___ ___ ___ ___ ___ ___ ___ ___ ___!
1   12 5   12 3   12 3 7 9 4 1 7

Watch out! Some letters are not used in the riddle!

Find the quotient.

A	B	C	D
144 ÷ 12 = ____	14 ÷ 7 = ____	56 ÷ 7 = ____	42 ÷ 6 = ____
G	**I**	**J**	**K**
0 ÷ 4 = ____	11 ÷ 11 = ____	20 ÷ 2 = ____	36 ÷ 6 = ____
M	**N**	**O**	**P**
25 ÷ 5 = ____	9 ÷ 3 = ____	16 ÷ 4 = ____	0 ÷ 3 = ____
R	**S**	**T**	**U**
63 ÷ 7 = ____	60 ÷ 6 = ____	12 ÷ 2 = ____	72 ÷ 9 = ____
V	**W**	**X**	**Y**
121 ÷ 11 = ____	100 ÷ 10 = ____	48 ÷ 6 = ____	44 ÷ 4 = ____

Use Halving to Divide

For 32 ÷ 4, you know that 4 is 2 × 2.

To divide by 4, divide by 2 first. 　　32 ÷ 2 = 16
Then divide by 2 again. 　　　　　　16 ÷ 2 = 8

So, 32 ÷ 4 = **8** .

16 ÷ 2 [array] 32 ÷ 2

Use halving to divide. Draw an array to help you.

a) 44 ÷ 4

Divide by 2. _____

Divide by 2 again. _____

So, 44 ÷ 4 = _____ .

b) 36 ÷ 4

Divide by 2. _____

Divide by 2 again. _____

So, 36 ÷ 4 = _____ .

c) 28 ÷ 4

Divide by 2. _____

Divide by 2 again. _____

So, 28 ÷ 4 = _____ .

d) 48 ÷ 4

Divide by 2. _____

Divide by 2 again. _____

So, 48 ÷ 4 = _____ .

e) 20 ÷ 4

Divide by 2. _____

Divide by 2 again. _____

So, 20 ÷ 4 = _____ .

f) 24 ÷ 4

Divide by 2. _____

Divide by 2 again. _____

So, 24 ÷ 4 = _____ .

Use Halving to Divide

Use repeated halving to divide. Hint: To divide by 8, divide by 2, divide by 2 again, then divide by 2 again.

a) 24 ÷ 8

Divide by 2. _____

Divide by 2. _____

Divide by 2. _____

So, 24 ÷ 8 = _____ .

b) 40 ÷ 8

Divide by 2. _____

Divide by 2. _____

Divide by 2. _____

So, 40 ÷ 8 = _____ .

c) 64 ÷ 8

Divide by 2. _____

Divide by 2. _____

Divide by 2. _____

So, 64 ÷ 8 = _____ .

d) 56 ÷ 8

Divide by 2. _____

Divide by 2. _____

Divide by 2. _____

So, 56 ÷ 8 = _____ .

e) 48 ÷ 8

Divide by 2. _____

Divide by 2. _____

Divide by 2. _____

So, 48 ÷ 8 = _____ .

f) 32 ÷ 8

Divide by 2. _____

Divide by 2. _____

Divide by 2. _____

So, 32 ÷ 8 = _____ .

BRAIN STRETCH

Seth says he can use repeated halving to divide 96 ÷ 8? Is he correct?
Show all the steps.

Use Blocks to Divide

Pam wants to divide 86 cards among her 4 friends.
She uses blocks to model division. 86 = 8 tens and 6 ones

Pam shares the tens, then shares the ones.
There are 2 tens and 1 one in each group. 2 ones are left.
So, 86 ÷ 4 = 21 with 2 left over.

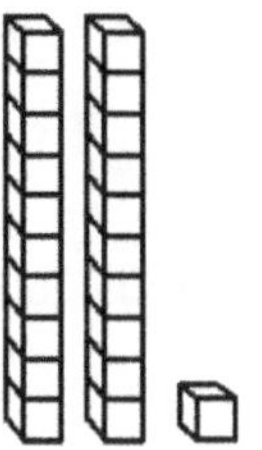 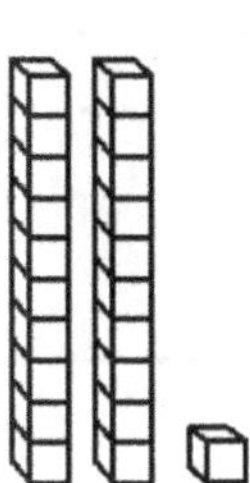 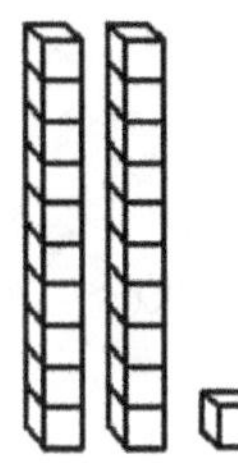 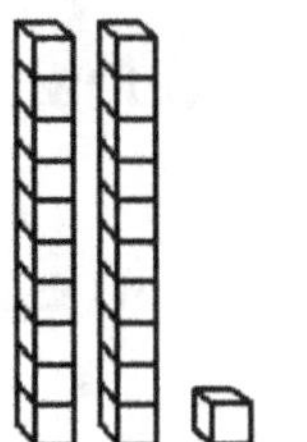

She uses long division to check.   4 groups ⟶ 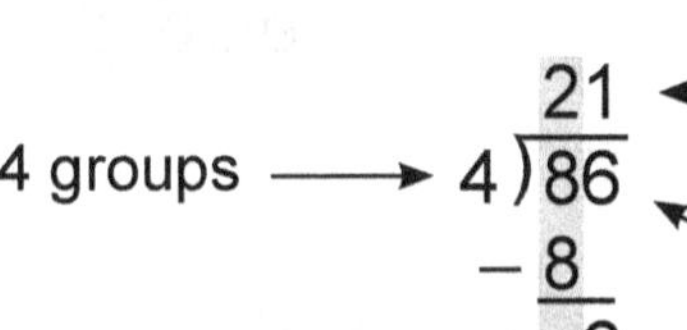

```
        21  ⟵ 2 tens in each group
             1 one in each group
  4)86  ⟵ 86 cards
  − 8
    6
  − 4
    2  ⟵ 2 ones left over
```

Use blocks to model division. Then divide.

```
      24
  2)48
  − 4
    8
  − 8
    0
```

2 groups

2 tens and 4 ones

in each group

a) 3)69

_____ groups

____

in each group

b) 5)75

_____ groups

____

in each group

Use Blocks to Divide

Divide. Write how many are left over.

a) 5)67

______ groups

__________ in each group

______ left over

b) 4)89

______ groups

__________ in each group

______ left over

c) 3)92

______ groups

__________ in each group

______ left over

d) 2)45

______ groups

__________ in each group

______ left over

e) 4)78

______ groups

__________ in each group

______ left over

f) 6)39

______ groups

__________ in each group

______ left over

Jenny plants 88 trees in 4 rows. How many trees are in each row? Use a model to help you solve the problem.

Divide Multiples of 10, 100, and 1,000

Divide: $4{,}000 \div 8 =$

Think: 40 ones $\div 8 = \underline{5}$ ones $= \mathbf{\underline{5}}$

40 tens $\div 8 = \underline{5}$ tens $= \mathbf{\underline{50}}$

40 hundreds $\div 8 = \underline{5}$ hundreds $= \mathbf{\underline{500}}$

So, $\mathbf{4{,}000 \div 8 = 500}$.

Use division facts and patterns to help you divide.

a) $9 \div 3 =$ _______

$90 \div 3 =$ _______

$900 \div 3 =$ _______

$9{,}000 \div 3 =$ _______

b) $16 \div 4 =$ _______

$160 \div 4 =$ _______

$1{,}600 \div 4 =$ _______

$16{,}000 \div 4 =$ _______

c) $6 \div 2 =$ _______

$60 \div 2 =$ _______

$600 \div 2 =$ _______

$6{,}000 \div 2 =$ _______

d) $8 \div 8 =$ _______

$80 \div 8 =$ _______

$800 \div 8 =$ _______

$8{,}000 \div 8 =$ _______

e) $10 \div 5 =$ _______

$100 \div 5 =$ _______

$1{,}000 \div 5 =$ _______

$10{,}000 \div 5 =$ _______

f) $25 \div 5 =$ _______

$250 \div 5 =$ _______

$2{,}500 \div 5 =$ _______

$25{,}000 \div 5 =$ _______

Divide Multiples of 10, 100, and 1,000

Use division facts and patterns to help you divide.

a) $4 \div 2 =$ ______

  $40 \div 2 =$ ______

  $400 \div 2 =$ ______

  $4{,}000 \div 2 =$ ______

b) $16 \div 4 =$ ______

  $160 \div 4 =$ ______

  $1{,}600 \div 4 =$ ______

  $16{,}000 \div 4 =$ ______

c) $6 \div 2 =$ ______

  $60 \div 2 =$ ______

  $600 \div 2 =$ ______

  $6{,}000 \div 2 =$ ______

d) $49 \div 7 =$ ______

  $490 \div 7 =$ ______

  $4{,}900 \div 7 =$ ______

  $49{,}000 \div 7 =$ ______

e) $18 \div 9 =$ ______

  $180 \div 9 =$ ______

  $1{,}800 \div 9 =$ ______

  $18{,}000 \div 9 =$ ______

f) $24 \div 6 =$ ______

  $240 \div 6 =$ ______

  $2{,}400 \div 6 =$ ______

  $24{,}000 \div 6 =$ ______

g) $36 \div 6 =$ ______

  $360 \div 6 =$ ______

  $3{,}600 \div 6 =$ ______

  $36{,}000 \div 6 =$ ______

h) $20 \div 4 =$ ______

  $200 \div 4 =$ ______

  $2{,}000 \div 4 =$ ______

  $20{,}000 \div 4 =$ ______

i) $50 \div 5 =$ ______

  $500 \div 5 =$ ______

  $5{,}000 \div 5 =$ ______

  $50{,}000 \div 5 =$ ______

Divide Multiples of 10, 100, and 1,000

Use division facts and patterns to help you divide.

a) 48 ÷ 12 = _______

480 ÷ 12 = _______

4,800 ÷ 12 = _______

48,000 ÷ 12 = _______

b) 54 ÷ 9 = _______

540 ÷ 9 = _______

5,400 ÷ 9 = _______

54,000 ÷ 9 = _______

c) 32 ÷ 8 = _______

320 ÷ 8 = _______

3,200 ÷ 8 = _______

32,000 ÷ 8 = _______

Divide.

70 ÷ 7 = _______

2,400 ÷ 6 = _______

3,000 ÷ 3 = _______

80 ÷ 2 = _______

6,300 ÷ 7 = _______

7,000 ÷ 7 = _______

200 ÷ 2 = _______

6,400 ÷ 8 = _______

20 ÷ 4 = _______

200 ÷ 4 = _______

4,800 ÷ 4 = _______

60 ÷ 3 = _______

720 ÷ 9 = _______

140 ÷ 7 = _______

5,600 ÷ 8 = _______

8,100 ÷ 9 = _______

50 ÷ 10 = _______

350 ÷ 7 = _______

5,000 ÷ 5 = _______

120 ÷ 3 = _______

6,000 ÷ 3 = _______

Math Riddle: Divide Multiples of 10, 100, and 1,000

How did the rabbit try to make gold soup?

__ __ __ __ __ __ __ __ __ __ __ __ __ __ __ __
900 400   60 30 400 800   1,200 90 400 1,000 1,200 20   500 40 60 50

__ __ __ __ __ __ __!
700 10 50 50 40 1,200 30

Watch out! Some letters are not used in the riddle!

Find the quotient.

A	C	D	E
7)70	8)5600	8)6400	6)2400

F	G	H	I
4)2000	7)700	9)8100	9)720

M	N	O	R
3)240	3)3000	4)160	10)500

S	T	U	W
2)60	4)4800	7)420	7)630

Y	Z
3)60	5)500

Math Riddle: Division Fun

I am a wind-up toy that can walk. I am made from tinplate and stand just 6 inches tall, who am I?

$$\overline{10} \quad \overline{11} \; \overline{12} \qquad \overline{5} \; \overline{4} \; \overline{7} \qquad \overline{2} \; \overline{10} \; \overline{9} \; \overline{400} \; \overline{5} \qquad \overline{9} \; \overline{6} \; \overline{60} \; \overline{6} \; \overline{5}$$

$$\overline{5} \; \overline{6} \; \overline{20} \; , \qquad \overline{70} \; \overline{10} \; \overline{70} \; \overline{70} \; \overline{10} \; \overline{8} \; \overline{3} \; \overline{5} \; !$$

Watch out! Some letters are not used in the riddle!

Find the quotient.

A	B	C	D
$7\overline{)77}$	$100\overline{)6000}$	$3\overline{)45}$	$2\overline{)64}$
E	**F**	**G**	**H**
$9\overline{)63}$	$9\overline{)18}$	$40\overline{)600}$	$2\overline{)8}$
I	**J**	**K**	**L**
$12\overline{)120}$	$10\overline{)140}$	$100\overline{)5000}$	$10\overline{)700}$
M	**O**	**P**	**R**
$5\overline{)60}$	$6\overline{)36}$	$10\overline{)80}$	$5\overline{)45}$
S	**T**	**U**	**Y**
$10\overline{)4000}$	$4\overline{)20}$	$7\overline{)21}$	$10\overline{)200}$

Math Riddle: Division Fun

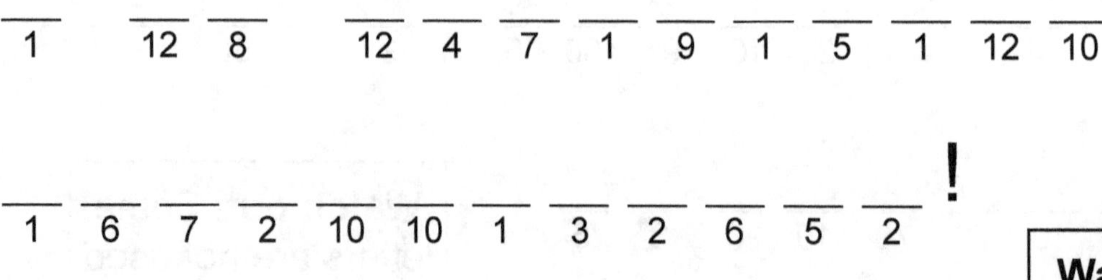

$\overline{}\ \overline{}\ \overline{}\quad \overline{}\ \overline{}\ \overline{}\ \overline{}\ \overline{}\ \overline{}\ \overline{}\ \overline{}\ \overline{}\ \overline{}$

1   12 8   12 4 7 1 9 1 5 1 12 10

1 6 7 2 10 10 1 3 2 6 5 2 !

Watch out! Some letters are not used in the riddle!

Find the quotient.

A	B	C	D
2)24	2)22	12)60	10)140
E	**F**	**G**	**H**
3)6	8)72	8)24	100)1500
I	**L**	**M**	**N**
4)4	10)100	2)16	1)6
O	**R**	**T**	
9)99	7)28	7)49	

Division with Remainders

Use multiplication and addition to find an answer with a remainder.

To find 22 ÷ 3, think of a factor of 3 that is close to 22.
Think: 7 × 3 = **21**
So you know there are 3 groups of 7 in 22.

But how do you get 22? Count up from 21 to find the remainder.
21 + **1** = 22, so the remainder is 1.

So, 22 ÷ 3 = **7 Remainder 1, or 7 R 1**.

Solve. Use multiplication and addition to find an answer with a remainder.

a) 19 ÷ 2 = _______

Think: 9 × _____ = _18_

_18_ + _____ = _19_

So, 19 ÷ 2 = _______.

b) 13 ÷ 2 = _______

Think: _____ × _____ = _____

_____ + _____ = _____

So, 13 ÷ 2 = _______.

c) 67 ÷ 7 = _______

Think: _____ × _____ = _____

_____ + _____ = _____

So, 67 ÷ 7 = _______.

d) 55 ÷ 6 = _______

Think: _____ × _____ = _____

_____ + _____ = _____

So, 55 ÷ 6 = _______.

e) 44 ÷ 6 = _______

Think: _____ × _____ = _____

_____ + _____ = _____

So, 44 ÷ 6 = _______.

f) 73 ÷ 8 = _______

Think: _____ × _____ = _____

_____ + _____ = _____

So, 73 ÷ 8 = _______.

Division with Remainders

Solve. Use multiplication and addition to find an answer with a remainder.

a) 15 ÷ 2 = _______

Think: _____ × _____ = _____

_____ + _____ = _____

So, 15 ÷ 2 = _______.

b) 25 ÷ 2 = _______

Think: _____ × _____ = _____

_____ + _____ = _____

So, _____ ÷ _____ = _______.

c) 47 ÷ 7 = _______

Think: _____ × _____ = _____

_____ + _____ = _____

So, _____ ÷ _____ = _______.

d) 63 ÷ 6 = _______

Think: _____ × _____ = _____

_____ + _____ = _____

So, _____ ÷ _____ = _______.

e) 54 ÷ 7 = _______

Think: _____ × _____ = _____

_____ + _____ = _____

So, _____ ÷ _____ = _______.

f) 36 ÷ 8 = _______

Think: _____ × _____ = _____

_____ + _____ = _____

So, _____ ÷ _____ = _______.

g) 78 ÷ 8 = _______

Think: _____ × _____ = _____

_____ + _____ = _____

So, _____ ÷ _____ = _______.

h) 85 ÷ 9 = _______

Think: _____ × _____ = _____

_____ + _____ = _____

So, _____ ÷ _____ = _______.

Division with Remainders

Solve. Use multiplication and addition to find an answer with a remainder.

a) 37 ÷ 5 = _______

Think: _____ × _____ = _____

_____ + _____ = _____

So, 37 ÷ 5 = _______.

b) 29 ÷ 4 = _______

Think: _____ × _____ = _____

_____ + _____ = _____

So, _____ ÷ _____ = _______.

c) 89 ÷ 7 = _______

Think: _____ × _____ = _____

_____ + _____ = _____

So, _____ ÷ _____ = _______.

d) 57 ÷ 6 = _______

Think: _____ × _____ = _____

_____ + _____ = _____

So, _____ ÷ _____ = _______.

e) 25 ÷ 3 = _______

Think: _____ × _____ = _____

_____ + _____ = _____

So, _____ ÷ _____ = _______.

f) 44 ÷ 8 = _______

Think: _____ × _____ = _____

_____ + _____ = _____

So, _____ ÷ _____ = _______.

g) 63 ÷ 5 = _______

Think: _____ × _____ = _____

_____ + _____ = _____

So, _____ ÷ _____ = _______.

h) 57 ÷ 9 = _______

Think: _____ × _____ = _____

_____ + _____ = _____

So, _____ ÷ _____ = _______.

Divide a Two-Digit Number by a One-Digit Number

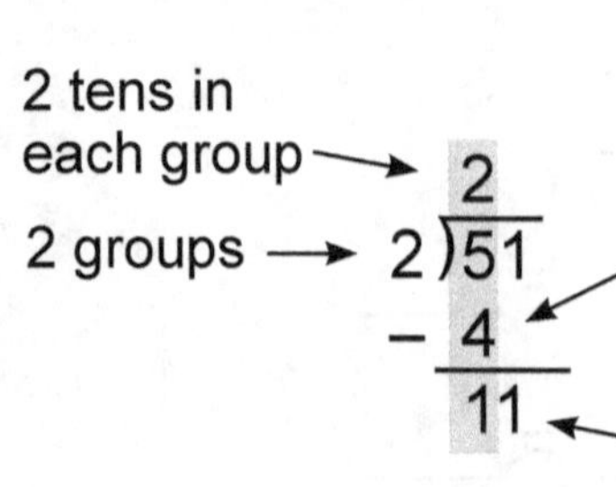

2 tens in each group →

2 groups → 2)51
− 4
11 ←

Step 1: Divide to find how many tens can go in each group.

Step 2: Multiply: 4 tens are placed. Subtract: 1 ten is left. So, 1 ten and 1 one are left. Write 1 beside the 1 ten.

25 ← 5 ones in each group
2)51
− 4
11
− 10
1

Step 3: Divide to find how many ones can go in each group.

Step 4: Multiply 10 ones are placed. Subtract to find that 1 one is left. So, the answer is 25 R 1.

R means remainder.

Find the quotient. Hint: The answer in division is called the **quotient**.

a) 8)65

b) 7)10

c) 5)47

d) 3)66

e) 7)67

f) 2)77

g) 4)18

h) 5)27

Divide. Hint: As you work, line up the tens and ones. Shade the tens column orange. Shade the ones column yellow.

a) $7\overline{)77}$

b) $7\overline{)98}$

c) $2\overline{)61}$

d) $3\overline{)13}$

e) $3\overline{)26}$

f) $2\overline{)50}$

g) $3\overline{)75}$

h) $2\overline{)39}$

i) $4\overline{)84}$

j) $3\overline{)19}$

k) $5\overline{)90}$

l) $7\overline{)53}$

Divide a Two-Digit Number by a One-Digit Number

Divide. Hint: As you work, line up the tens and ones. Shade the tens column orange. Shade the ones column yellow.

a) 7⟌44

b) 2⟌86

c) 5⟌39

d) 2⟌41

e) 3⟌54

f) 6⟌91

g) 4⟌65

h) 2⟌57

i) 2⟌49

j) 6⟌25

k) 7⟌90

l) 3⟌87

Divide a Two-Digit Number by a One-Digit Number

Divide. Hint: As you work, line up the tens and ones. Shade the tens column orange. Shade the ones column yellow.

a) $8\overline{)79}$ b) $3\overline{)48}$ c) $2\overline{)85}$ d) $2\overline{)64}$

e) $3\overline{)68}$ f) $7\overline{)39}$ g) $6\overline{)46}$ h) $8\overline{)96}$

i) $5\overline{)69}$ j) $9\overline{)77}$ k) $5\overline{)65}$ l) $4\overline{)57}$

Divide Multi-Digit Numbers

Divide.

Hint: There are fewer hundreds than groups. So, the division starts with the tens.

a) 2)991

b) 2)345

c) 9)603

d) 7)238

e) 6)366

f) 8)890

g) 5)659

h) 4)537

i) 3)254

j) 3)187

Divide Multi-Digit Numbers

Divide. Hint: As you work, line up the hundreds, tens, and ones. Shade the tens column orange. Shade the ones column yellow. Shade the hundreds column green.

a) $4\overline{)527}$

b) $5\overline{)293}$

c) $6\overline{)749}$

d) $8\overline{)274}$

e) $3\overline{)943}$

f) $9\overline{)471}$

g) $6\overline{)762}$

h) $5\overline{)142}$

i) $3\overline{)656}$

j) $2\overline{)431}$

k) $2\overline{)825}$

l) $4\overline{)488}$

Divide Multi-Digit Numbers

Divide. Hint: As you work, line up the hundreds, tens, and ones. Shade the tens column orange. Shade the ones column yellow. Shade the hundreds column green.

a) $5\overline{)760}$ b) $7\overline{)259}$ c) $4\overline{)749}$ d) $8\overline{)368}$

e) $3\overline{)652}$ f) $9\overline{)369}$ g) $6\overline{)444}$ h) $5\overline{)755}$

i) $7\overline{)637}$ j) $2\overline{)857}$ k) $2\overline{)111}$ l) $3\overline{)488}$

Estimate a Quotient

Use **compatible numbers** to estimate a quotient.
Compatible numbers are numbers that divide evenly.

Estimate: 243 ÷ 6.   Divide 6 into the first 2 digits. How many 6s are in 24?

Think: 24 ÷ 6 = 4
        240 ÷ 6 = 40   Since it is an estimate, write 0 for the ones digit.
The estimated quotient is 40.

Use compatible numbers to estimate the quotient. Show your work.

a) 5)355

_____ ÷ _____ = _____

_____ ÷ _____ = _____

b) 3)246

_____ ÷ _____ = _____

_____ ÷ _____ = _____

c) 4)284

_____ ÷ _____ = _____

_____ ÷ _____ = _____

d) 2)128

_____ ÷ _____ = _____

_____ ÷ _____ = _____

e) 6)468

_____ ÷ _____ = _____

_____ ÷ _____ = _____

f) 7)581

_____ ÷ _____ = _____

_____ ÷ _____ = _____

Estimate a Quotient

Estimate: 312 ÷ 4

Think: What multiples of 4 are close to 31?

28 is too low   32 is close to 31   36 is too high

32 ÷ 4 = 8   So, try 8.

320 ÷ 4 = 80   Write 0 for the ones digit.

The estimated quotient is 80.

Estimate the quotient. Show your work.

a) 3)‾143‾

b) 4)‾254‾

c) 5)‾224‾

_____ ÷ _____ = _____

_____ ÷ _____ = _____

d) 6)‾431‾

e) 8)‾634‾

f) 5)‾365‾

_____ ÷ _____ = _____

_____ ÷ _____ = _____

Division Fact Fun—Test 1

#		#	
1.	12 ÷ 12 = _____	21.	0 ÷ 5 = _____
2.	22 ÷ 11 = _____	22.	66 ÷ 6 = _____
3.	90 ÷ 10 = _____	23.	35 ÷ 7 = _____
4.	121 ÷ 11 = _____	24.	48 ÷ 8 = _____
5.	40 ÷ 8 = _____	25.	88 ÷ 8 = _____
6.	7 ÷ 7 = _____	26.	0 ÷ 10 = _____
7.	0 ÷ 6 = _____	27.	77 ÷ 11 = _____
8.	35 ÷ 5 = _____	28.	60 ÷ 12 = _____
9.	44 ÷ 4 = _____	29.	4 ÷ 1 = _____
10.	12 ÷ 3 = _____	30.	108 ÷ 9 = _____
11.	8 ÷ 2 = _____	31.	24 ÷ 2 = _____
12.	3 ÷ 1 = _____	32.	42 ÷ 7 = _____
13.	132 ÷ 12 = _____	33.	15 ÷ 3 = _____
14.	55 ÷ 11 = _____	34.	12 ÷ 6 = _____
15.	120 ÷ 10 = _____	35.	30 ÷ 5 = _____
16.	99 ÷ 9 = _____	36.	8 ÷ 4 = _____
17.	72 ÷ 8 = _____	37.	20 ÷ 10 = _____
18.	6 ÷ 6 = _____	38.	96 ÷ 12 = _____
19.	20 ÷ 5 = _____	39.	33 ÷ 3 = _____
20.	48 ÷ 4 = _____	40.	16 ÷ 2 = _____

Number Correct

_____
40

Division Fact Fun—Test 2

1. $6 \div 2 = $ _____
2. $0 \div 3 = $ _____
3. $28 \div 4 = $ _____
4. $50 \div 5 = $ _____
5. $72 \div 6 = $ _____
6. $0 \div 7 = $ _____
7. $16 \div 8 = $ _____
8. $54 \div 9 = $ _____
9. $80 \div 10 = $ _____
10. $88 \div 11 = $ _____
11. $120 \div 12 = $ _____
12. $9 \div 1 = $ _____
13. $3 \div 3 = $ _____
14. $55 \div 5 = $ _____
15. $63 \div 7 = $ _____
16. $27 \div 9 = $ _____
17. $66 \div 11 = $ _____
18. $12 \div 2 = $ _____
19. $24 \div 4 = $ _____
20. $48 \div 6 = $ _____

21. $60 \div 10 = $ _____
22. $42 \div 6 = $ _____
23. $70 \div 7 = $ _____
24. $45 \div 9 = $ _____
25. $14 \div 2 = $ _____
26. $5 \div 1 = $ _____
27. $108 \div 12 = $ _____
28. $33 \div 11 = $ _____
29. $18 \div 9 = $ _____
30. $32 \div 8 = $ _____
31. $77 \div 7 = $ _____
32. $30 \div 6 = $ _____
33. $5 \div 5 = $ _____
34. $36 \div 4 = $ _____
35. $6 \div 3 = $ _____
36. $10 \div 2 = $ _____
37. $0 \div 1 = $ _____
38. $72 \div 12 = $ _____
39. $40 \div 10 = $ _____
40. $0 \div 8 = $ _____

Number Correct

_____
40

Division Fact Fun—Test 3

1. $12 \div 1 =$ _____

2. $22 \div 2 =$ _____

3. $9 \div 3 =$ _____

4. $16 \div 4 =$ _____

5. $40 \div 5 =$ _____

6. $54 \div 6 =$ _____

7. $14 \div 7 =$ _____

8. $64 \div 8 =$ _____

9. $72 \div 9 =$ _____

10. $10 \div 10 =$ _____

11. $110 \div 11 =$ _____

12. $36 \div 12 =$ _____

13. $25 \div 5 =$ _____

14. $60 \div 6 =$ _____

15. $28 \div 7 =$ _____

16. $88 \div 8 =$ _____

17. $9 \div 9 =$ _____

18. $30 \div 10 =$ _____

19. $0 \div 11 =$ _____

20. $144 \div 12 =$ _____

21. $2 \div 2 =$ _____

22. $36 \div 4 =$ _____

23. $18 \div 6 =$ _____

24. $24 \div 8 =$ _____

25. $100 \div 10 =$ _____

26. $84 \div 12 =$ _____

27. $27 \div 3 =$ _____

28. $15 \div 5 =$ _____

29. $49 \div 7 =$ _____

30. $81 \div 9 =$ _____

31. $1 \div 1 =$ _____

32. $44 \div 11 =$ _____

33. $0 \div 4 =$ _____

34. $36 \div 3 =$ _____

35. $20 \div 2 =$ _____

36. $6 \div 1 =$ _____

37. $36 \div 6 =$ _____

38. $55 \div 5 =$ _____

39. $4 \div 4 =$ _____

40. $18 \div 3 =$ _____

Number Correct

_____ / 40

Division Fact Fun—Test 4

1. $7 \div 1 =$ _____

2. $20 \div 2 =$ _____

3. $6 \div 3 =$ _____

4. $20 \div 4 =$ _____

5. $35 \div 5 =$ _____

6. $48 \div 6 =$ _____

7. $77 \div 7 =$ _____

8. $80 \div 8 =$ _____

9. $108 \div 9 =$ _____

10. $100 \div 10 =$ _____

11. $22 \div 11 =$ _____

12. $144 \div 12 =$ _____

13. $55 \div 5 =$ _____

14. $18 \div 6 =$ _____

15. $42 \div 7 =$ _____

16. $64 \div 8 =$ _____

17. $81 \div 9 =$ _____

18. $30 \div 10 =$ _____

19. $0 \div 11 =$ _____

20. $36 \div 12 =$ _____

21. $20 \div 5 =$ _____

22. $16 \div 4 =$ _____

23. $42 \div 6 =$ _____

24. $32 \div 8 =$ _____

25. $10 \div 10 =$ _____

26. $108 \div 12 =$ _____

27. $21 \div 3 =$ _____

28. $10 \div 5 =$ _____

29. $49 \div 7 =$ _____

30. $9 \div 9 =$ _____

31. $0 \div 1 =$ _____

32. $99 \div 11 =$ _____

33. $32 \div 4 =$ _____

34. $36 \div 3 =$ _____

35. $22 \div 2 =$ _____

36. $2 \div 1 =$ _____

37. $36 \div 6 =$ _____

38. $25 \div 5 =$ _____

39. $40 \div 4 =$ _____

40. $15 \div 3 =$ _____

Number Correct

_____
40

Division Fact Fun—Test 5

1.	$12 \div 12 = $ _____	**21.**	$0 \div 5 = $ _____
2.	$22 \div 11 = $ _____	**22.**	$66 \div 6 = $ _____
3.	$90 \div 10 = $ _____	**23.**	$45 \div 9 = $ _____
4.	$121 \div 11 = $ _____	**24.**	$48 \div 8 = $ _____
5.	$40 \div 8 = $ _____	**25.**	$88 \div 8 = $ _____
6.	$7 \div 7 = $ _____	**26.**	$0 \div 10 = $ _____
7.	$0 \div 6 = $ _____	**27.**	$77 \div 11 = $ _____
8.	$35 \div 5 = $ _____	**28.**	$60 \div 12 = $ _____
9.	$44 \div 4 = $ _____	**29.**	$4 \div 1 = $ _____
10.	$12 \div 3 = $ _____	**30.**	$108 \div 9 = $ _____
11.	$8 \div 2 = $ _____	**31.**	$24 \div 2 = $ _____
12.	$3 \div 1 = $ _____	**32.**	$42 \div 7 = $ _____
13.	$132 \div 12 = $ _____	**33.**	$15 \div 3 = $ _____
14.	$55 \div 11 = $ _____	**34.**	$12 \div 6 = $ _____
15.	$120 \div 10 = $ _____	**35.**	$30 \div 5 = $ _____
16.	$99 \div 9 = $ _____	**36.**	$8 \div 4 = $ _____
17.	$72 \div 8 = $ _____	**37.**	$20 \div 10 = $ _____
18.	$6 \div 6 = $ _____	**38.**	$96 \div 12 = $ _____
19.	$20 \div 5 = $ _____	**39.**	$33 \div 3 = $ _____
20.	$48 \div 4 = $ _____	**40.**	$16 \div 2 = $ _____

Number Correct

_____
40

Division Fact Fun—Test 6

1. $80 \div 4 =$ _____
2. $180 \div 2 =$ _____
3. $3,000 \div 6 =$ _____
4. $40 \div 4 =$ _____
5. $6,000 \div 5 =$ _____
6. $240 \div 6 =$ _____
7. $5,600 \div 7 =$ _____
8. $960 \div 8 =$ _____
9. $70,000 \div 10 =$ _____
10. $1,100 \div 10 =$ _____
11. $11,000 \div 11 =$ _____
12. $7,200 \div 12 =$ _____
13. $450 \div 5 =$ _____
14. $6,600 \div 6 =$ _____
15. $840 \div 7 =$ _____
16. $80 \div 8 =$ _____
17. $63,000 \div 9 =$ _____
18. $5,000 \div 10 =$ _____
19. $990 \div 11 =$ _____
20. $480 \div 12 =$ _____
21. $100 \div 5 =$ _____
22. $1,200 \div 4 =$ _____
23. $48,000 \div 6 =$ _____
24. $5,600 \div 8 =$ _____
25. $90 \div 10 =$ _____
26. $1,200 \div 12 =$ _____
27. $90 \div 3 =$ _____
28. $2,500 \div 5 =$ _____
29. $350 \div 7 =$ _____
30. $99,000 \div 9 =$ _____
31. $48,000 \div 4 =$ _____
32. $880 \div 11 =$ _____
33. $2,400 \div 4 =$ _____
34. $600 \div 3 =$ _____
35. $1,400 \div 2 =$ _____
36. $250 \div 5 =$ _____
37. $36,000 \div 6 =$ _____
38. $60 \div 5 =$ _____
39. $30 \div 5 =$ _____
40. $150 \div 3 =$ _____

Number Correct

_____
40

Division Table

The numbers in the dark border down the left side are the **quotients**.
The numbers in the dark border across the top are the **divisors**.
The numbers inside the table are the **dividends**.
Try it! To find the quotient for 72 ÷ 6, for example, find 6 in the divisor border and place a finger from your right hand on the 6.
Then slide your finger down the 6 column until you come to the number 72.
Keep your right finger on the 72 and place a finger from your left hand beside it on the same row.
Slide your left finger to the left along that row, toward the quotient border.
The number in the dark square at the end of the row is the quotient.
So, 72 ÷ 6 = 12.

Divisor

	0	1	2	3	4	5	6	7	8	9	10	11	12
0	0	0	0	0	0	0	0	0	0	0	0	0	0
1	0	1	2	3	4	5	6	7	8	9	10	11	12
2	0	2	4	6	8	10	12	14	16	18	20	22	24
3	0	3	6	9	12	15	18	21	24	27	30	33	36
4	0	4	8	12	16	20	24	28	32	36	40	44	48
5	0	5	10	15	20	25	30	35	40	45	50	55	60
6	0	6	12	18	24	30	36	42	48	54	60	66	72
7	0	7	14	21	28	35	42	49	56	63	70	77	84
8	0	8	16	24	32	40	48	56	64	72	80	88	96
9	0	9	18	27	36	45	54	63	72	81	90	99	108
10	0	10	20	30	40	50	60	70	80	90	100	110	120
11	0	11	22	33	44	55	66	77	88	99	110	121	132
12	0	12	24	36	48	60	72	84	96	108	120	132	144

Quotient (left border label)

WONDERFUL WORK!

Name

Answers

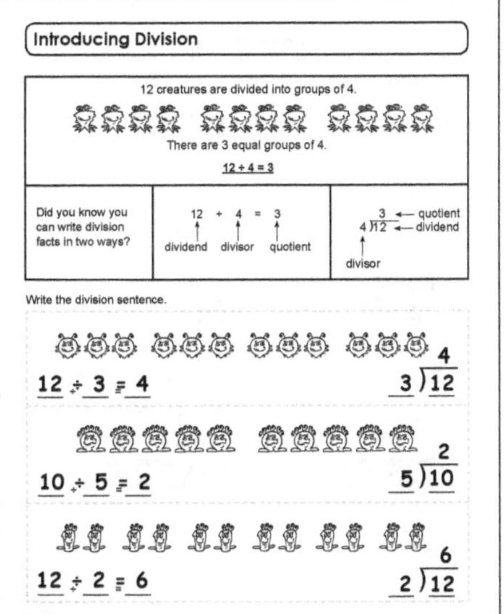

Introducing Division (page 3)

Write the division sentence.

15 ÷ 5 = 3   5)15   3

9 ÷ 3 = 3   3)9   3

14 ÷ 2 = 7   2)14   7

16 ÷ 4 = 4   4)16   4

12 ÷ 2 = 6   2)12   6

3

Introducing Division (page 4)

Write the division sentence.

20 ÷ 4 = 5   4)20   5

16 ÷ 8 = 2   8)16   2

14 ÷ 7 = 2   7)14   2

10 ÷ 2 = 5   2)10   5

12 ÷ 3 = 4   3)12   4

4

Introducing Division (page 5)

Use a circle to divide into groups. Complete the division sentence.

Divide 10 creatures into groups of 5.
2 groups   10 ÷ 5 = 2

Divide 18 creatures into groups of 6.
3 groups   18 ÷ 6 = 3

Divide 8 creatures into groups of 2.
4 groups   8 ÷ 2 = 4

Divide 12 creatures into groups of 4.
3 groups   12 ÷ 4 = 3

5

Introducing Division (page 6)

Use a circle to divide into groups. Complete the division sentence.

Divide 15 creatures into groups of 5.
3 groups   15 ÷ 5 = 3

Divide 9 creatures into groups of 3.
3 groups   9 ÷ 3 = 3

Divide 14 creatures into groups of 7.
2 groups   14 ÷ 7 = 2

Divide 16 creatures into groups of 4.
4 groups   16 ÷ 4 = 4

6

Divide by Skip Counting (page 7)

3 + 3 + 3 + 3 + 3 + 3 = 18
18 ÷ 3 =
It takes 6 skips of 3 to reach 18.   18 ÷ 3 = 6

Skip count on the number line to divide. Write the answer.

4 + 4 + 4 + 4 = 16
16 ÷ 4 =
It takes 4 skips of 4 to reach 16.   16 ÷ 4 = 4

3 + 3 + 3 + 3 + 3 = 15
15 ÷ 3 =
It takes 5 skips of 3 to reach 15.   15 ÷ 3 = 5

7

Divide by Skip Counting (page 8)

Skip count on the number line to divide. Write the answer.

5 + 5 + 5 + 5 = 20
20 ÷ 5 =
It takes 4 skips of 5 to reach 20.   20 ÷ 5 = 4

5 + 5 + 5 = 15
15 ÷ 5 =
It takes 3 skips of 5 to reach 15.   15 ÷ 5 = 3

4 + 4 + 4 = 12
12 ÷ 4 =
It takes 3 skips of 4 to reach 12.   12 ÷ 4 = 3

8

Divide by Skip Counting (page 9)

Skip count on the number line to divide. Write the answer.

2 + 2 + 2 + 2 + 2 + 2 + 2 + 2 = 16
16 ÷ 2 =
It takes 8 skips of 2 to reach 16.   16 ÷ 2 = 8

3 + 3 + 3 + 3 + 3 + 3 = 18
18 ÷ 3 =
It takes 6 skips of 3 to reach 18.   18 ÷ 3 = 6

4 + 4 + 4 + 4 + 4 = 20
20 ÷ 4 =
It takes 5 skips of 4 to reach 20.   20 ÷ 4 = 5

9

Relate Multiplication to Division

Use the array to complete each number sentence.

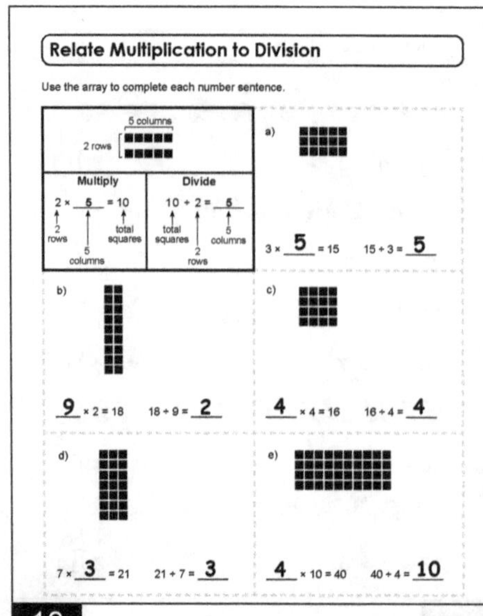

a)

$3 \times 5 = 15$ $15 \div 3 = 5$

b)

c)

$9 \times 2 = 18$ $18 \div 9 = 2$

$4 \times 4 = 16$ $16 \div 4 = 4$

d)

e)

$7 \times 3 = 21$ $21 \div 7 = 3$

$4 \times 10 = 40$ $40 \div 4 = 10$

10

Relate Multiplication to Division

Use the array to complete each number sentence.

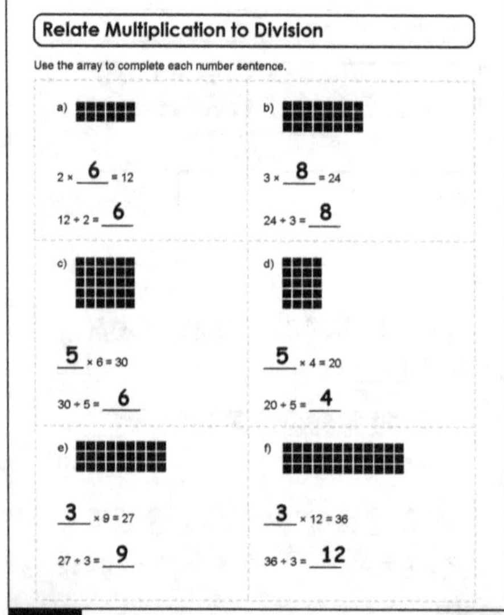

a)

$2 \times 6 = 12$

$12 \div 2 = 6$

b)

$3 \times 8 = 24$

$24 \div 3 = 8$

c)

$5 \times 6 = 30$

$30 \div 5 = 6$

d)

$5 \times 4 = 20$

$20 \div 5 = 4$

e)

$3 \times 9 = 27$

$27 \div 3 = 9$

f)

$3 \times 12 = 36$

$36 \div 3 = 12$

11

Relate Multiplication to Division

Use the array to complete each number sentence.

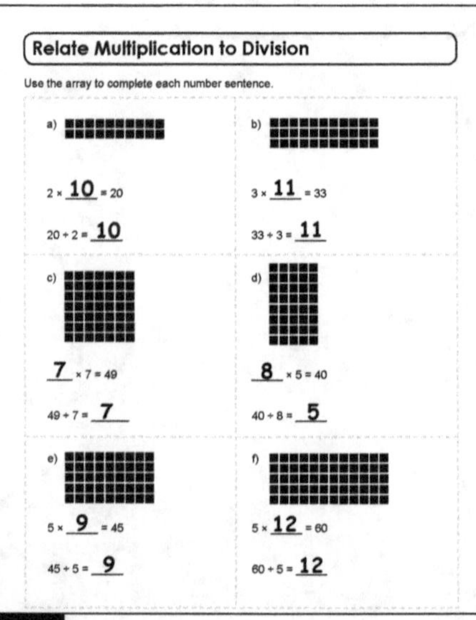

a)

$2 \times 10 = 20$

$20 \div 2 = 10$

b)

$3 \times 11 = 33$

$33 \div 3 = 11$

c)

$7 \times 7 = 49$

$49 \div 7 = 7$

d)

$8 \times 5 = 40$

$40 \div 8 = 5$

e)

$5 \times 9 = 45$

$45 \div 5 = 9$

f)

$5 \times 12 = 60$

$60 \div 5 = 12$

12

Use an Array to Find a Quotient

Draw an array to help you find each quotient.

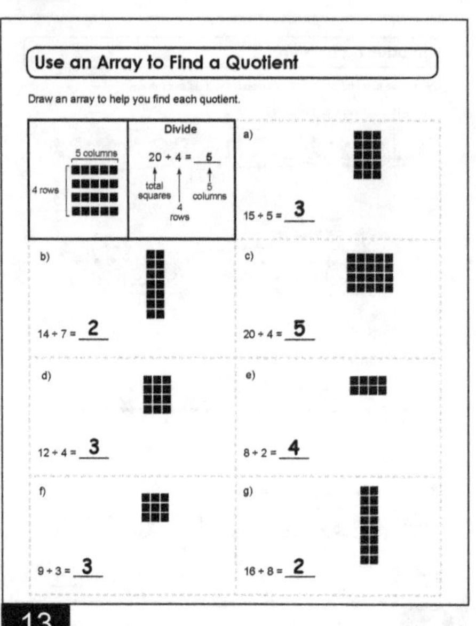

a)

$15 \div 5 = 3$

b)

c)

$14 \div 7 = 2$

$20 \div 4 = 5$

d)

e)

$12 \div 4 = 3$

$8 \div 2 = 4$

f)

g)

$9 \div 3 = 3$

$16 \div 8 = 2$

13

Use an Array to Find a Quotient

Draw an array to help you find each quotient.

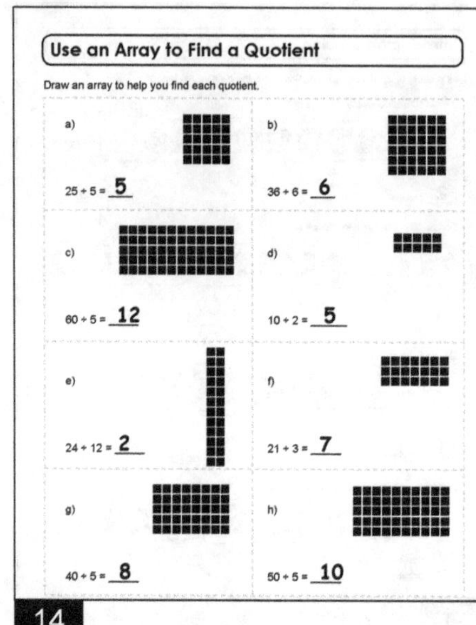

a)

$25 \div 5 = 5$

b)

$36 \div 6 = 6$

c)

$60 \div 5 = 12$

d)

$10 \div 2 = 5$

e)

$24 \div 12 = 2$

f)

$21 \div 3 = 7$

g)

$40 \div 5 = 8$

h)

$50 \div 5 = 10$

14

Use an Array to Find a Quotient

Draw an array to help you find each quotient.

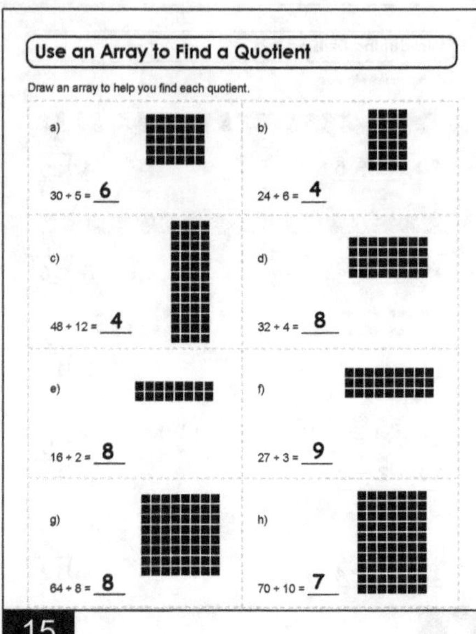

a)

$30 \div 5 = 6$

b)

$24 \div 6 = 4$

c)

$48 \div 12 = 4$

d)

$32 \div 4 = 8$

e)

$16 \div 2 = 8$

f)

$27 \div 3 = 9$

g)

$64 \div 8 = 8$

h)

$70 \div 10 = 7$

15

Relate Multiplication to Division

Use the multiplication fact to find each quotient.

a) $11 \times 3 = 33$

$33 \div 11 = 3$

b) $9 \times 7 = 63$

$63 \div 7 = 9$

c) $6 \times 7 = 42$

$42 \div 6 = 7$

d) $4 \times 10 = 40$

$40 \div 4 = 10$

e) $9 \times 5 = 45$

$45 \div 9 = 5$

f) $2 \times 8 = 16$

$16 \div 2 = 8$

g) $9 \times 9 = 81$

$81 \div 9 = 9$

h) $7 \times 11 = 77$

$77 \div 7 = 11$

i) $8 \times 1 = 8$

$8 \div 8 = 1$

j) $8 \times 5 = 40$

$40 \div 8 = 5$

k) $9 \times 12 = 108$

$108 \div 9 = 12$

l) $11 \times 11 = 121$

$121 \div 11 = 11$

16

Relate Multiplication to Division

Use the multiplication fact to find each quotient.

a) $2 \times 3 = 6$

$6 \div 2 = 3$

b) $6 \times 9 = 54$

$54 \div 6 = 9$

c) $2 \times 8 = 16$

$16 \div 2 = 8$

d) $4 \times 7 = 28$

$28 \div 4 = 7$

e) $7 \times 12 = 84$

$84 \div 7 = 12$

f) $5 \times 6 = 30$

$30 \div 5 = 6$

g) $9 \times 2 = 18$

$18 \div 9 = 2$

h) $8 \times 11 = 88$

$88 \div 8 = 11$

i) $9 \times 1 = 9$

$9 \div 9 = 1$

j) $6 \times 8 = 48$

$48 \div 6 = 8$

k) $9 \times 11 = 99$

$99 \div 9 = 11$

l) $11 \times 10 = 110$

$110 \div 11 = 10$

17

Use Related Multiplication Facts to Divide with 0 and 1

The quotient is always 1 when any number other than 0 is divided by itself.	The quotient is always the same as the dividend when any number is divided by 1.
For example, $5 \div 5 = 1$.	For example, $8 \div 1 = 8$.
Think of a related multiplication fact.	Think of a related multiplication fact.
$5 \times 1 = 5$, so $5 \div 5 = 1$	$8 \times 1 = 8$, so $8 \div 1 = 8$

The quotient is always 0 when 0 is divided by any number other than 0.

For example, $0 \div 3 = 0$.

Think of a related multiplication fact.

$3 \times 0 = 0$, so $0 \div 3 = 0$

You cannot divide any number by 0.

Divide.

$0 \div 7 = 0$	$12 \div 12 = 1$	$10 \div 1 = 10$	$0 \div 6 = 0$
$5 \div 1 = 5$	$0 \div 4 = 0$	$3 \div 3 = 1$	$7 \div 7 = 1$
$0 \div 1 = 0$	$11 \div 1 = 11$	$0 \div 8 = 0$	$6 \div 1 = 6$
$8 \div 8 = 1$	$0 \div 9 = 0$	$9 \div 1 = 9$	$0 \div 2 = 0$

18

19. Divide by 2

Draw a line from the division sentence to the correct quotient. Hint: Practice skip counting by 2s.

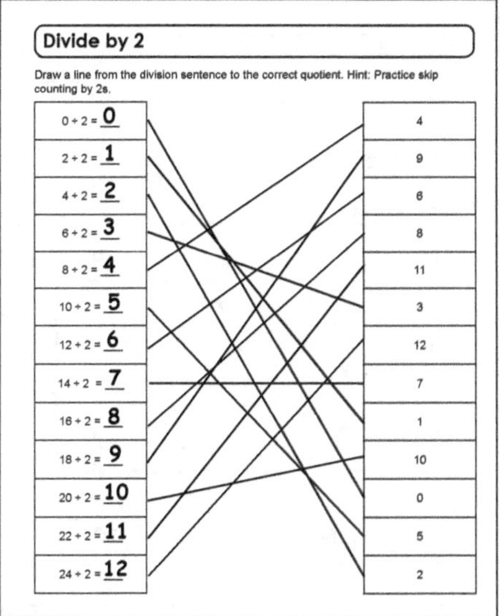

0 ÷ 2 = 0		4
2 ÷ 2 = 1		9
4 ÷ 2 = 2		6
6 ÷ 2 = 3		8
8 ÷ 2 = 4		11
10 ÷ 2 = 5		3
12 ÷ 2 = 6		12
14 ÷ 2 = 7		7
16 ÷ 2 = 8		1
18 ÷ 2 = 9		10
20 ÷ 2 = 10		0
22 ÷ 2 = 11		5
24 ÷ 2 = 12		2

20. Math Riddle: Divide by 2

What is a polar bear's favorite food?

I C E   B U R G E R S !
4 8 11   1 2 7 0 11 7 6

Watch out! Some letters are not used in the riddle!

Find the quotient.

A: 18 ÷ 2 = 9	B: 2 ÷ 2 = 1	C: 16 ÷ 2 = 8
E: 22 ÷ 2 = 11	F: 6 ÷ 2 = 3	G: 0 ÷ 2 = 0
I: 8 ÷ 2 = 4	M: 10 ÷ 2 = 5	N: 24 ÷ 2 = 12
R: 14 ÷ 2 = 7	S: 12 ÷ 2 = 6	U: 4 ÷ 2 = 2

Find the missing dividend.

4 ÷ 2 = 2	16 ÷ 2 = 8	20 ÷ 2 = 10	2 ÷ 2 = 1
22 ÷ 2 = 11	12 ÷ 2 = 6	24 ÷ 2 = 12	0 ÷ 2 = 0

21. Divide by 3

Draw a line from the division sentence to the correct quotient. Hint: Practice skip counting by 3s.

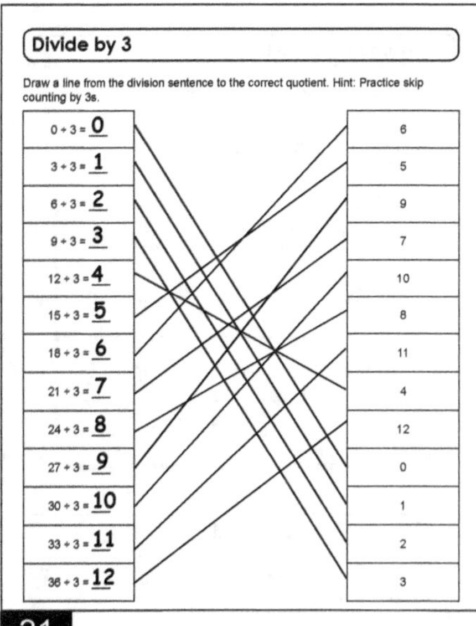

0 ÷ 3 = 0		6
3 ÷ 3 = 1		5
6 ÷ 3 = 2		9
9 ÷ 3 = 3		7
12 ÷ 3 = 4		10
15 ÷ 3 = 5		8
18 ÷ 3 = 6		11
21 ÷ 3 = 7		4
24 ÷ 3 = 8		12
27 ÷ 3 = 9		0
30 ÷ 3 = 10		1
33 ÷ 3 = 11		2
36 ÷ 3 = 12		3

22. Math Riddle: Divide by 3

What kind of hats do penguins wear?

I C E   C A P S !
7 8 11   8 5 6 4

Watch out! Some letters are not used in the riddle!

Find the quotient.

A: 15 ÷ 3 = 5	B: 3 ÷ 3 = 1	C: 24 ÷ 3 = 8
E: 33 ÷ 3 = 11	H: 6 ÷ 3 = 2	I: 21 ÷ 3 = 7
M: 27 ÷ 3 = 9	N: 36 ÷ 3 = 12	O: 30 ÷ 3 = 10
P: 18 ÷ 3 = 6	S: 12 ÷ 3 = 4	T: 9 ÷ 3 = 3

Find the missing dividend.

18 ÷ 3 = 6	24 ÷ 3 = 8	15 ÷ 3 = 5	30 ÷ 3 = 10
21 ÷ 3 = 7	27 ÷ 3 = 9	36 ÷ 3 = 12	9 ÷ 3 = 3

23. Divide by 1, 2, and 3

Draw a line from the division sentence to the correct quotient. Color division facts with odd quotients red. Color the division facts with even quotients blue.

0 ÷ 1 = 0	3	9 ÷ 3 = 3
12 ÷ 2 = 6	9	5 ÷ 1 = 5
15 ÷ 3 = 5	7	21 ÷ 3 = 7
11 ÷ 1 = 11	5	24 ÷ 2 = 12
20 ÷ 2 = 10	10	1 ÷ 1 = 1
36 ÷ 3 = 12	4	22 ÷ 2 = 11
4 ÷ 2 = 2	12	12 ÷ 3 = 4
14 ÷ 2 = 7	2	10 ÷ 1 = 10
3 ÷ 3 = 1	6	16 ÷ 2 = 8
6 ÷ 2 = 3	11	18 ÷ 3 = 6
8 ÷ 2 = 4	1	27 ÷ 3 = 9
16 ÷ 2 = 8	0	4 ÷ 2 = 2
18 ÷ 2 = 9	8	0 ÷ 3 = 0

24. Divide by 1, 2, and 3

Find the quotient.

30 ÷ 3 = 10	10 ÷ 2 = 5	21 ÷ 3 = 7	1 ÷ 1 = 1
22 ÷ 2 = 11	36 ÷ 3 = 12	12 ÷ 1 = 12	8 ÷ 2 = 4
10 ÷ 1 = 10	24 ÷ 3 = 8	24 ÷ 2 = 12	8 ÷ 1 = 8
18 ÷ 3 = 6	6 ÷ 2 = 3	12 ÷ 3 = 4	11 ÷ 1 = 11
12 ÷ 2 = 6	7 ÷ 1 = 7	14 ÷ 2 = 7	33 ÷ 3 = 11
9 ÷ 3 = 3	5 ÷ 1 = 5	27 ÷ 3 = 9	0 ÷ 1 = 0
4 ÷ 2 = 2	6 ÷ 3 = 2	9 ÷ 1 = 9	2 ÷ 2 = 1

25. Divide by 1, 2, and 3

Find the quotient.

a) $1\overline{)6}=6$	b) $3\overline{)3}=1$	c) $2\overline{)12}=6$	d) $1\overline{)4}=4$
e) $3\overline{)24}=8$	f) $2\overline{)16}=8$	g) $2\overline{)8}=4$	h) $3\overline{)30}=10$
i) $2\overline{)4}=2$	j) $1\overline{)5}=5$	k) $3\overline{)12}=4$	l) $2\overline{)22}=11$
m) $2\overline{)18}=9$	n) $3\overline{)27}=9$	o) $1\overline{)8}=8$	p) $2\overline{)10}=5$

26. Math Riddle: Divide by 1, 2, and 3

Where do astronauts keep their lunch?

I N   A   L A U N C H   B O X !
7 10   8   4 8 9 10 12 3   11 6 1

Watch out! Some letters are not used in the riddle!

Find the quotient.

A: $3\overline{)24}=8$	B: $3\overline{)33}=11$	C: $3\overline{)36}=12$	D: $2\overline{)28}=14$
E: $3\overline{)6}=2$	F: $1\overline{)6}=6$	G: $2\overline{)4}=2$	H: $3\overline{)9}=3$
I: $2\overline{)14}=7$	J: $2\overline{)30}=15$	K: $1\overline{)2}=2$	L: $3\overline{)12}=4$
M: $2\overline{)12}=6$	N: $3\overline{)30}=10$	O: $2\overline{)10}=5$	R: $3\overline{)18}=6$
S: $3\overline{)6}=2$	U: $3\overline{)27}=9$	V: $3\overline{)15}=5$	X: $1\overline{)1}=1$

27. Divide by 4

Draw a line from the division sentence to the correct quotient. Hint: Practice skip counting by 4s.

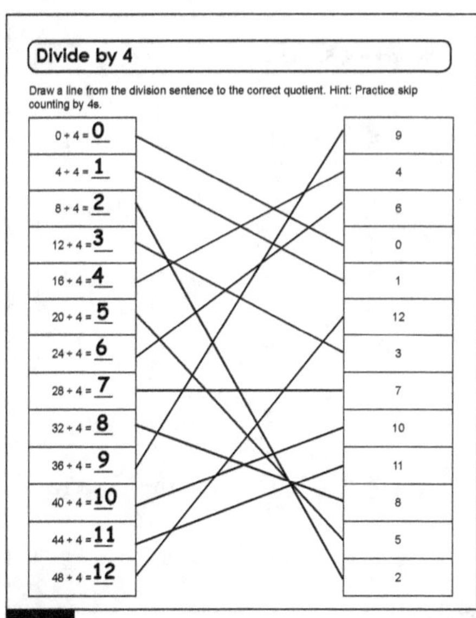

0 ÷ 4 = 0		9
4 ÷ 4 = 1		4
8 ÷ 4 = 2		6
12 ÷ 4 = 3		0
16 ÷ 4 = 4		1
20 ÷ 4 = 5		12
24 ÷ 4 = 6		3
28 ÷ 4 = 7		7
32 ÷ 4 = 8		10
36 ÷ 4 = 9		11
40 ÷ 4 = 10		8
44 ÷ 4 = 11		5
48 ÷ 4 = 12		2

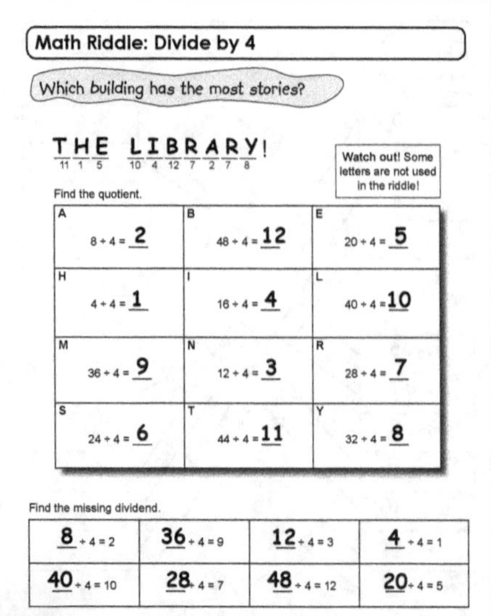

Math Riddle: Divide by 4

Which building has the most stories?

T H E   L I B R A R Y !
11 1 5   10 4 12 7 2 7 8

Watch out! Some letters are not used in the riddle!

Find the quotient.

A	B	E
8 ÷ 4 = **2**	48 ÷ 4 = **12**	20 ÷ 4 = **5**
H 4 ÷ 4 = **1**	**I** 16 ÷ 4 = **4**	**L** 40 ÷ 4 = **10**
M 36 ÷ 4 = **9**	**N** 12 ÷ 4 = **3**	**R** 28 ÷ 4 = **7**
S 24 ÷ 4 = **6**	**T** 44 ÷ 4 = **11**	**Y** 32 ÷ 4 = **8**

Find the missing dividend.

8 ÷ 4 = 2	**36** ÷ 4 = 9	**12** ÷ 4 = 3	**4** ÷ 4 = 1
40 ÷ 4 = 10	**28** ÷ 4 = 7	**48** ÷ 4 = 12	**20** ÷ 4 = 5

`28`

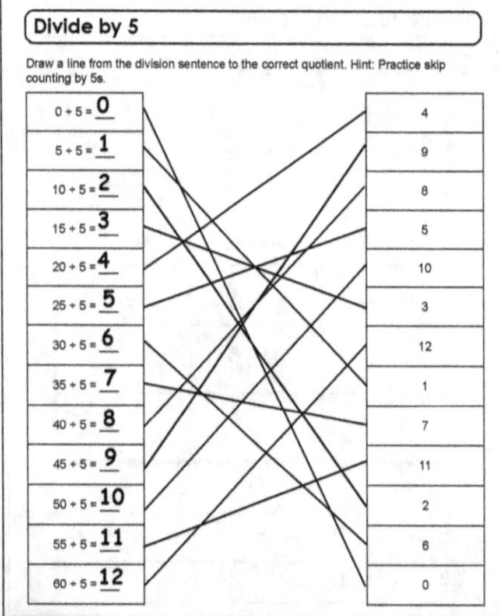

Divide by 5

Draw a line from the division sentence to the correct quotient. Hint: Practice skip counting by 5s.

0 ÷ 5 = **0**	4
5 ÷ 5 = **1**	9
10 ÷ 5 = **2**	8
15 ÷ 5 = **3**	5
20 ÷ 5 = **4**	10
25 ÷ 5 = **5**	3
30 ÷ 5 = **6**	12
35 ÷ 5 = **7**	1
40 ÷ 5 = **8**	7
45 ÷ 5 = **9**	11
50 ÷ 5 = **10**	2
55 ÷ 5 = **11**	6
60 ÷ 5 = **12**	0

`29`

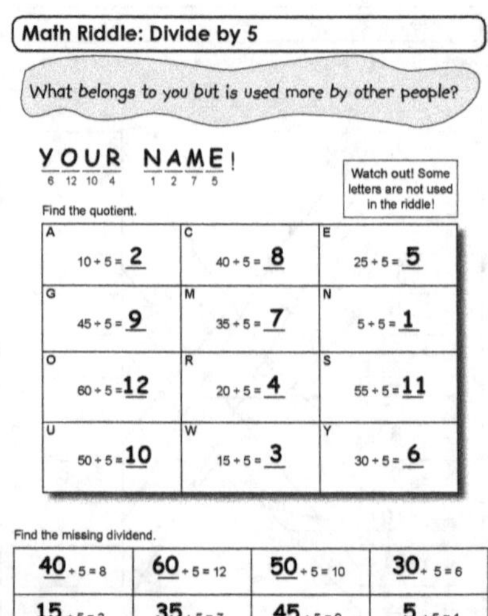

Math Riddle: Divide by 5

What belongs to you but is used more by other people?

Y O U R   N A M E !
6 12 10 4   1 2 7 5

Watch out! Some letters are not used in the riddle!

Find the quotient.

A	C	E
10 ÷ 5 = **2**	40 ÷ 5 = **8**	25 ÷ 5 = **5**
G 45 ÷ 5 = **9**	**M** 35 ÷ 5 = **7**	**N** 5 ÷ 5 = **1**
O 60 ÷ 5 = **12**	**R** 20 ÷ 5 = **4**	**S** 55 ÷ 5 = **11**
U 50 ÷ 5 = **10**	**W** 15 ÷ 5 = **3**	**Y** 30 ÷ 5 = **6**

Find the missing dividend.

40 ÷ 5 = 8	**60** ÷ 5 = 12	**50** ÷ 5 = 10	**30** ÷ 5 = 6
15 ÷ 5 = 3	**35** ÷ 5 = 7	**45** ÷ 5 = 9	**5** ÷ 5 = 1

`30`

Divide by 6

Draw a line from the division sentence to the correct quotient. Hint: Practice skip counting by 6s.

0 ÷ 6 = **0**	8
6 ÷ 6 = **1**	9
12 ÷ 6 = **2**	6
18 ÷ 6 = **3**	5
24 ÷ 6 = **4**	11
30 ÷ 6 = **5**	7
36 ÷ 6 = **6**	12
42 ÷ 6 = **7**	3
48 ÷ 6 = **8**	10
54 ÷ 6 = **9**	4
60 ÷ 6 = **10**	0
66 ÷ 6 = **11**	1
72 ÷ 6 = **12**	2

`31`

Math Riddle: Divide by 6

What did the tornado say to the sports car?

L E T ' S   G O   F O R   A   S P I N !
7 8 10 11   6 9   12 9 4   3   11 5 2 1

Find the quotient.

A	E	F
18 ÷ 6 = **3**	48 ÷ 6 = **8**	72 ÷ 6 = **12**
G 36 ÷ 6 = **6**	**I** 12 ÷ 6 = **2**	**L** 42 ÷ 6 = **7**
N 6 ÷ 6 = **1**	**O** 54 ÷ 6 = **9**	**P** 30 ÷ 6 = **5**
R 24 ÷ 6 = **4**	**S** 66 ÷ 6 = **11**	**T** 60 ÷ 6 = **10**

Find the missing dividend.

60 ÷ 6 = 10	**48** ÷ 6 = 8	**66** ÷ 6 = 11	**30** ÷ 6 = 5
54 ÷ 6 = 9	**24** ÷ 6 = 4	**42** ÷ 6 = 7	**18** ÷ 6 = 3

`32`

Divide by 4, 5, and 6

Draw a line from the division sentence to the correct quotient. Color division facts with odd quotients red. Color the division facts with even quotients blue.

0 ÷ 6 = **0**	7	10 ÷ 5 = **2**
60 ÷ 5 = **12**	9	28 ÷ 4 = **7**
8 ÷ 4 = **2**	4	20 ÷ 4 = **5**
66 ÷ 6 = **11**	5	0 ÷ 5 = **0**
20 ÷ 5 = **4**	12	32 ÷ 4 = **8**
36 ÷ 6 = **6**	3	24 ÷ 6 = **4**
6 ÷ 6 = **1**	10	50 ÷ 5 = **10**
35 ÷ 5 = **7**	2	44 ÷ 4 = **11**
12 ÷ 4 = **3**	0	48 ÷ 4 = **12**
54 ÷ 6 = **9**	8	45 ÷ 5 = **9**
40 ÷ 5 = **8**	1	6 ÷ 6 = **1**
40 ÷ 4 = **10**	6	24 ÷ 4 = **6**
30 ÷ 6 = **5**	11	15 ÷ 5 = **3**

`33`

Divide by 4, 5, and 6

Find the quotient.

32 ÷ 4 = **8**	5 ÷ 5 = **1**	66 ÷ 6 = **11**	36 ÷ 4 = **9**
25 ÷ 5 = **5**	36 ÷ 6 = **6**	4 ÷ 4 = **1**	0 ÷ 5 = **0**
12 ÷ 6 = **2**	24 ÷ 4 = **6**	35 ÷ 5 = **7**	6 ÷ 6 = **1**
16 ÷ 4 = **4**	45 ÷ 5 = **9**	54 ÷ 6 = **9**	12 ÷ 4 = **3**
10 ÷ 5 = **2**	18 ÷ 6 = **3**	28 ÷ 4 = **7**	15 ÷ 5 = **3**
24 ÷ 6 = **4**	48 ÷ 4 = **12**	50 ÷ 5 = **10**	72 ÷ 6 = **12**
0 ÷ 4 = **0**	20 ÷ 5 = **4**	48 ÷ 6 = **8**	8 ÷ 4 = **2**

`34`

Divide by 4, 5, and 6

Find the quotient.

a) 4)24 = **6**	b) 5)5 = **1**	c) 6)18 = **3**	d) 4)44 = **11**
e) 6)60 = **10**	f) 4)20 = **5**	g) 5)10 = **2**	h) 6)30 = **5**
i) 5)35 = **7**	j) 6)42 = **7**	k) 4)4 = **1**	l) 5)55 = **11**
m) 4)28 = **7**	n) 5)20 = **4**	o) 6)66 = **11**	p) 4)12 = **3**

`35`

Math Riddle: Divide by 4, 5, and 6

When does the Moon weigh the most?

W H E N   I T   I S   F U L L !
9 4 1 3   11 8   11 2   5 10 7 7

Watch out! Some letters are not used in the riddle!

Find the quotient.

E	F	G	H
1 6)6	**5** 5)25	**12** 6)72	**4** 5)20
I **11** 4)44	**K** **6** 5)30	**L** **7** 5)35	**M** **0** 5)0
N **3** 4)12	**O** **6** 4)24	**P** **12** 4)48	**S** **2** 5)10
T **8** 6)48	**U** **10** 5)50	**W** **9** 5)45	**X** **6** 6)36

`36`

37 — Divide by 7

Divide by 7

Draw a line from the division sentence to the correct quotient. Hint: Practice skip counting by 7s.

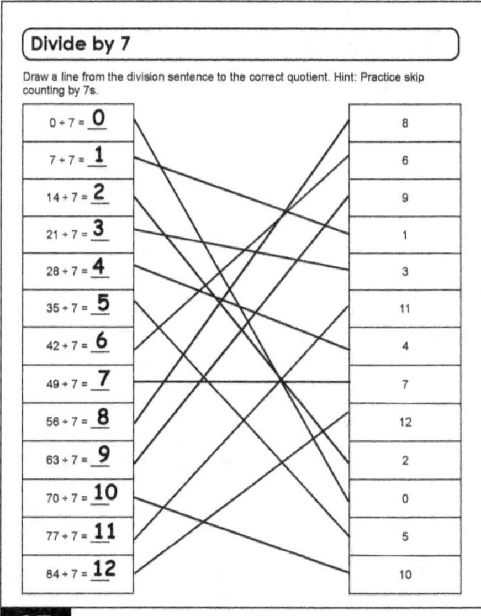

Division sentence	Quotient
0 ÷ 7 = **0**	8
7 ÷ 7 = **1**	6
14 ÷ 7 = **2**	9
21 ÷ 7 = **3**	1
28 ÷ 7 = **4**	3
35 ÷ 7 = **5**	11
42 ÷ 7 = **6**	4
49 ÷ 7 = **7**	7
56 ÷ 7 = **8**	12
63 ÷ 7 = **9**	2
70 ÷ 7 = **10**	0
77 ÷ 7 = **11**	5
84 ÷ 7 = **12**	10

38 — Math Riddle: Divide by 7

Math Riddle: Divide by 7

How did the robot make the number seven even?

Watch out! Some letters are not used in the riddle!

S H E   T O O K   O U T   T H E   S !
11 9 7   10 5 5 6   5 4 10   10 9 7   11

Find the quotient.

A 14 ÷ 7 = **2**	C 84 ÷ 7 = **12**	D 21 ÷ 7 = **3**
E 49 ÷ 7 = **7**	H 63 ÷ 7 = **9**	K 42 ÷ 7 = **6**
O 35 ÷ 7 = **5**	P 56 ÷ 7 = **8**	S 77 ÷ 7 = **11**
T 70 ÷ 7 = **10**	U 28 ÷ 7 = **4**	W 7 ÷ 7 = **1**

Find the missing dividend.

35 ÷ 7 = 5	**56** ÷ 7 = 8	**84** ÷ 7 = 12	**28** ÷ 7 = 4
70 ÷ 7 = 10	**14** ÷ 7 = 2	**42** ÷ 7 = 6	**21** ÷ 7 = 3

39 — Divide by 8

Divide by 8

Draw a line from the division sentence to the correct quotient. Hint: Practice skip counting by 8s.

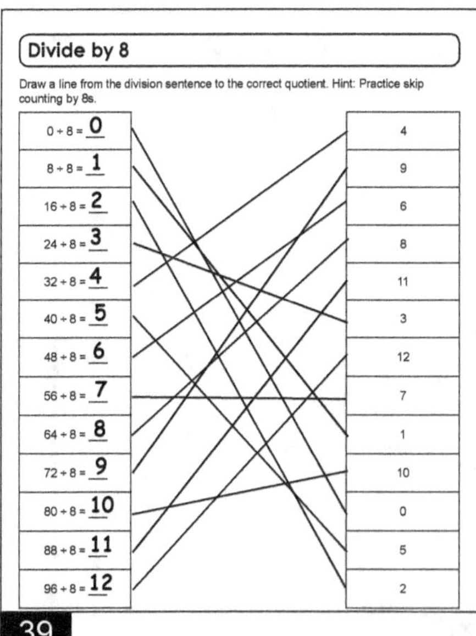

Division sentence	Quotient
0 ÷ 8 = **0**	4
8 ÷ 8 = **1**	9
16 ÷ 8 = **2**	6
24 ÷ 8 = **3**	8
32 ÷ 8 = **4**	11
40 ÷ 8 = **5**	3
48 ÷ 8 = **6**	12
56 ÷ 8 = **7**	7
64 ÷ 8 = **8**	1
72 ÷ 8 = **9**	10
80 ÷ 8 = **10**	0
88 ÷ 8 = **11**	5
96 ÷ 8 = **12**	2

40 — Math Riddle: Divide by 8

Math Riddle: Divide by 8

What has four legs but cannot walk?

A   C H A I R !
3   9 2 3 5 8

Watch out! Some letters are not used in the riddle!

Find the quotient.

A 24 ÷ 8 = **3**	B 48 ÷ 8 = **6**	C 72 ÷ 8 = **9**
E 32 ÷ 8 = **4**	H 16 ÷ 8 = **2**	I 40 ÷ 8 = **5**
J 96 ÷ 8 = **12**	K 56 ÷ 8 = **7**	L 80 ÷ 8 = **10**
P 88 ÷ 8 = **11**	Q 8 ÷ 8 = **1**	R 64 ÷ 8 = **8**

Find the missing dividend.

16 ÷ 8 = 2	**88** ÷ 8 = 11	**64** ÷ 8 = 8	**32** ÷ 8 = 4
80 ÷ 8 = 10	**24** ÷ 8 = 3	**72** ÷ 8 = 9	**96** ÷ 8 = 12

41 — Divide by 9

Divide by 9

Draw a line from the division sentence to the correct quotient. Hint: Practice skip counting by 9s.

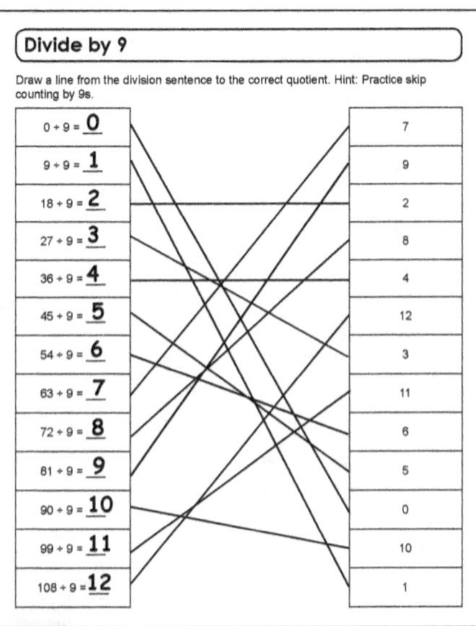

Division sentence	Quotient
0 ÷ 9 = **0**	7
9 ÷ 9 = **1**	9
18 ÷ 9 = **2**	2
27 ÷ 9 = **3**	8
36 ÷ 9 = **4**	4
45 ÷ 9 = **5**	12
54 ÷ 9 = **6**	3
63 ÷ 9 = **7**	11
72 ÷ 9 = **8**	6
81 ÷ 9 = **9**	5
90 ÷ 9 = **10**	0
99 ÷ 9 = **11**	10
108 ÷ 9 = **12**	1

42 — Math Riddle: Divide by 9

Math Riddle: Divide by 9

Where do fish like to sleep?

O N   A   S E A B E D !
6 10   4   1 2 4 5 2 9

Watch out! Some letters are not used in the riddle!

Find the quotient.

A 36 ÷ 9 = **4**	B 45 ÷ 9 = **5**	C 72 ÷ 9 = **8**
D 81 ÷ 9 = **9**	E 18 ÷ 9 = **2**	M 99 ÷ 9 = **11**
N 90 ÷ 9 = **10**	O 54 ÷ 9 = **6**	P 27 ÷ 9 = **3**
R 108 ÷ 9 = **12**	S 9 ÷ 9 = **1**	T 63 ÷ 9 = **7**

Find the missing dividend.

90 ÷ 9 = 10	**72** ÷ 9 = 8	**99** ÷ 9 = 11	**45** ÷ 9 = 5
81 ÷ 9 = 9	**36** ÷ 9 = 4	**63** ÷ 9 = 7	**27** ÷ 9 = 3

43 — Divide by 7, 8, and 9

Divide by 7, 8, and 9

Draw a line from the division sentence to the correct quotient. Color division facts with odd quotients red. Color the division facts with even quotients blue.

Column 1	Middle	Column 3
0 ÷ 9 = **0**	11	63 ÷ 7 = **9**
64 ÷ 8 = **8**	5	28 ÷ 7 = **4**
77 ÷ 7 = **11**	4	0 ÷ 8 = **0**
108 ÷ 9 = **12**	9	27 ÷ 9 = **3**
40 ÷ 8 = **5**	12	72 ÷ 9 = **8**
70 ÷ 7 = **10**	2	42 ÷ 7 = **6**
63 ÷ 9 = **7**	1	7 ÷ 7 = **1**
8 ÷ 8 = **1**	3	45 ÷ 9 = **5**
21 ÷ 7 = **3**	6	16 ÷ 8 = **2**
54 ÷ 9 = **6**	8	49 ÷ 7 = **7**
32 ÷ 8 = **4**	10	96 ÷ 8 = **12**
14 ÷ 7 = **2**	0	88 ÷ 8 = **11**
81 ÷ 9 = **9**	7	90 ÷ 9 = **10**

44 — Divide by 7, 8, and 9

Divide by 7, 8, and 9

Find the quotient.

35 ÷ 7 = **5**	8 ÷ 8 = **1**	108 ÷ 9 = **12**	70 ÷ 7 = **10**
24 ÷ 8 = **3**	45 ÷ 9 = **5**	21 ÷ 7 = **3**	0 ÷ 8 = **0**
9 ÷ 9 = **1**	56 ÷ 7 = **8**	32 ÷ 8 = **4**	81 ÷ 9 = **9**
14 ÷ 7 = **2**	64 ÷ 8 = **8**	54 ÷ 9 = **6**	0 ÷ 7 = **0**
16 ÷ 8 = **2**	90 ÷ 9 = **10**	28 ÷ 7 = **4**	48 ÷ 8 = **6**
63 ÷ 9 = **7**	42 ÷ 7 = **6**	56 ÷ 8 = **7**	72 ÷ 9 = **8**
49 ÷ 7 = **7**	80 ÷ 8 = **10**	99 ÷ 9 = **11**	84 ÷ 7 = **12**

45 — Divide by 7, 8, and 9

Divide by 7, 8, and 9

Find the quotient.

a) 7)49 = **7**	b) 8)96 = **12**	c) 8)24 = **3**	d) 9)18 = **2**
e) 8)64 = **8**	f) 9)99 = **11**	g) 7)56 = **8**	h) 8)40 = **5**
i) 7)63 = **9**	j) 8)56 = **7**	k) 9)90 = **10**	l) 7)70 = **10**
m) 9)54 = **6**	n) 7)42 = **6**	o) 8)48 = **6**	p) 9)27 = **3**

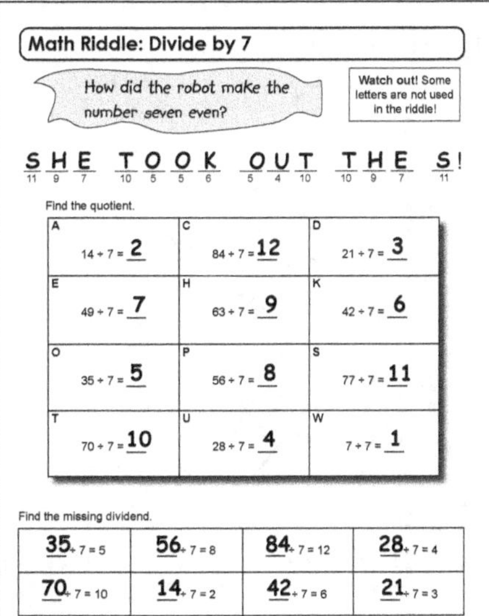

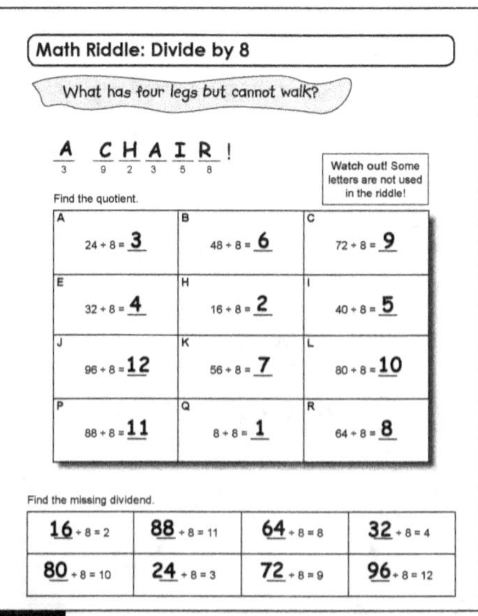

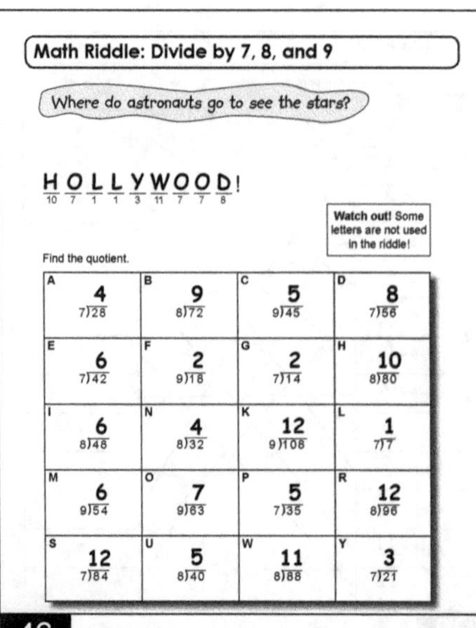

Math Riddle: Divide by 7, 8, and 9

Where do astronauts go to see the stars?

H O L L Y W O O D !
10 7 1 1 3 11 7 7 8

Watch out! Some letters are not used in the riddle!

Find the quotient.

A $7\overline{)28}$ = 4	B $8\overline{)72}$ = 9	C $9\overline{)45}$ = 5	D $7\overline{)56}$ = 8
E $7\overline{)42}$ = 6	F $9\overline{)18}$ = 2	G $7\overline{)14}$ = 2	H $8\overline{)80}$ = 10
I $8\overline{)48}$ = 6	N $8\overline{)32}$ = 4	K $9\overline{)108}$ = 12	L $7\overline{)7}$ = 1
M $9\overline{)54}$ = 6	O $9\overline{)63}$ = 7	P $7\overline{)35}$ = 5	R $8\overline{)96}$ = 12
S $7\overline{)84}$ = 12	U $8\overline{)40}$ = 5	W $8\overline{)88}$ = 11	Y $7\overline{)21}$ = 3

46

Divide by 10

Draw a line from the division sentence to the correct quotient. Hint: Practice skip counting by 10s.

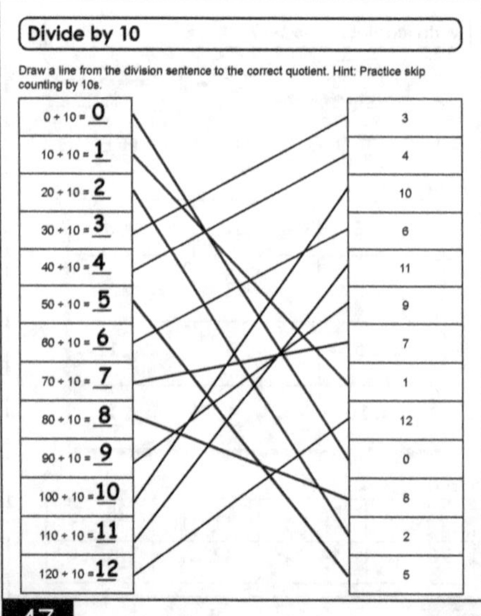

0 ÷ 10 = **0**		3
10 ÷ 10 = **1**		4
20 ÷ 10 = **2**		10
30 ÷ 10 = **3**		6
40 ÷ 10 = **4**		11
50 ÷ 10 = **5**		9
60 ÷ 10 = **6**		7
70 ÷ 10 = **7**		1
80 ÷ 10 = **8**		12
90 ÷ 10 = **9**		0
100 ÷ 10 = **10**		8
110 ÷ 10 = **11**		2
120 ÷ 10 = **12**		5

47

Math Riddle: Divide by 10

What do you call a famous fish?

A S T A R F I S H !
8 7 5 8 3 9 6 7 2

Watch out! Some letters are not used in the riddle!

Find the quotient.

A 80 ÷ 10 = **8**	B 40 ÷ 10 = **4**	E 120 ÷ 10 = **12**
F 90 ÷ 10 = **9**	G 110 ÷ 10 = **11**	H 20 ÷ 10 = **2**
I 80 ÷ 10 = **6**	J 100 ÷ 10 = **10**	R 30 ÷ 10 = **3**
S 70 ÷ 10 = **7**	T 50 ÷ 10 = **5**	Y 10 ÷ 10 = **1**

Find the missing dividend.

| **30** ÷ 10 = 3 | **80** ÷ 10 = 8 | **120** ÷ 10 = 12 | **60** ÷ 10 = 6 |
| **110** ÷ 10 = 11 | **50** ÷ 10 = 5 | **70** ÷ 10 = 7 | **90** ÷ 10 = 9 |

48

Divide by 11

Draw a line from the division sentence to the correct quotient. Hint: Practice skip counting by 11s.

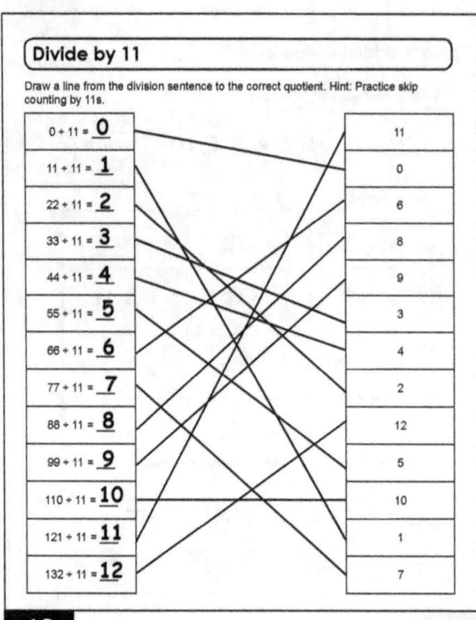

0 ÷ 11 = **0**		11
11 ÷ 11 = **1**		0
22 ÷ 11 = **2**		6
33 ÷ 11 = **3**		8
44 ÷ 11 = **4**		9
55 ÷ 11 = **5**		3
66 ÷ 11 = **6**		4
77 ÷ 11 = **7**		2
88 ÷ 11 = **8**		12
99 ÷ 11 = **9**		5
110 ÷ 11 = **10**		10
121 ÷ 11 = **11**		1
132 ÷ 11 = **12**		7

49

Math Riddle: Divide by 11

What animal is smarter than a talking dinosaur?

A S P E L L I N G   B E E !
3 8 2 4 1 1 10 12 7   11 4 4

Watch out! Some letters are not used in the riddle!

Find the quotient.

A 33 ÷ 11 = **3**	B 121 ÷ 11 = **11**	C 55 ÷ 11 = **5**
E 44 ÷ 11 = **4**	G 77 ÷ 11 = **7**	I 110 ÷ 11 = **10**
J 99 ÷ 11 = **9**	L 11 ÷ 11 = **1**	N 132 ÷ 11 = **12**
P 22 ÷ 11 = **2**	S 66 ÷ 11 = **6**	T 88 ÷ 11 = **8**

Find the missing dividend.

| **33** ÷ 11 = 3 | **44** ÷ 11 = 4 | **88** ÷ 11 = 8 | **132** ÷ 11 = 12 |
| **99** ÷ 11 = 9 | **110** ÷ 11 = 10 | **55** ÷ 11 = 5 | **22** ÷ 11 = 2 |

50

Divide by 12

Draw a line from the division sentence to the correct quotient. Hint: Practice skip counting by 12s.

0 ÷ 12 = **0**		10
12 ÷ 12 = **1**		8
24 ÷ 12 = **2**		6
36 ÷ 12 = **3**		12
48 ÷ 12 = **4**		5
60 ÷ 12 = **5**		9
72 ÷ 12 = **6**		11
84 ÷ 12 = **7**		0
96 ÷ 12 = **8**		2
108 ÷ 12 = **9**		4
120 ÷ 12 = **10**		1
132 ÷ 12 = **11**		7
144 ÷ 12 = **12**		3

51

Math Riddle: Divide by 12

What did the dog say to the flea?

S T O P   B U G G I N G   M E !
10 9 11 7   4 5 8 8 1 2 8   12 6

Watch out! Some letters are not used in the riddle!

Find the quotient.

A 36 ÷ 12 = **3**	B 48 ÷ 12 = **4**	E 72 ÷ 12 = **6**
I 12 ÷ 12 = **1**	G 96 ÷ 12 = **8**	M 144 ÷ 12 = **12**
N 24 ÷ 12 = **2**	O 132 ÷ 12 = **11**	P 84 ÷ 12 = **7**
S 120 ÷ 12 = **10**	T 108 ÷ 12 = **9**	U 60 ÷ 12 = **5**

Find the missing dividend.

| **132** ÷ 12 = 11 | **24** ÷ 12 = 2 | **108** ÷ 12 = 9 | **72** ÷ 12 = 6 |
| **60** ÷ 12 = 5 | **96** ÷ 12 = 8 | **84** ÷ 12 = 7 | **48** ÷ 12 = 4 |

52

Divide by 10, 11, and 12

Draw a line from the division sentence to the correct quotient. Color division facts with odd quotients red. Color the division facts with even quotients blue.

121 ÷ 11 = **11**	7		40 ÷ 10 = **4**	
60 ÷ 12 = **5**	9		72 ÷ 12 = **6**	
80 ÷ 10 = **8**	4		22 ÷ 11 = **2**	
99 ÷ 11 = **9**	5		10 ÷ 10 = **1**	
24 ÷ 12 = **2**	12		36 ÷ 12 = **3**	
100 ÷ 10 = **10**	3		121 ÷ 11 = **11**	
11 ÷ 11 = **1**	10		110 ÷ 11 = **10**	
0 ÷ 12 = **0**	2		108 ÷ 12 = **9**	
60 ÷ 10 = **6**	0		55 ÷ 11 = **5**	
132 ÷ 11 = **12**	8		84 ÷ 12 = **7**	
48 ÷ 12 = **4**	1		0 ÷ 10 = **0**	
30 ÷ 10 = **3**	6		88 ÷ 11 = **8**	
77 ÷ 11 = **7**	11		144 ÷ 12 = **12**	

53

Divide by 10, 11, and 12

Find the quotient.

30 ÷ 10 = **3**	110 ÷ 11 = **10**	108 ÷ 12 = **9**	50 ÷ 10 = **5**
55 ÷ 11 = **5**	36 ÷ 12 = **3**	90 ÷ 10 = **9**	0 ÷ 11 = **0**
144 ÷ 12 = **12**	80 ÷ 10 = **8**	22 ÷ 11 = **2**	48 ÷ 12 = **4**
100 ÷ 10 = **10**	44 ÷ 11 = **4**	84 ÷ 12 = **7**	120 ÷ 10 = **12**
33 ÷ 11 = **3**	60 ÷ 12 = **5**	20 ÷ 10 = **2**	88 ÷ 11 = **8**
24 ÷ 12 = **2**	70 ÷ 10 = **7**	11 ÷ 11 = **1**	72 ÷ 12 = **6**
40 ÷ 10 = **4**	66 ÷ 11 = **6**	96 ÷ 12 = **8**	10 ÷ 10 = **1**

54

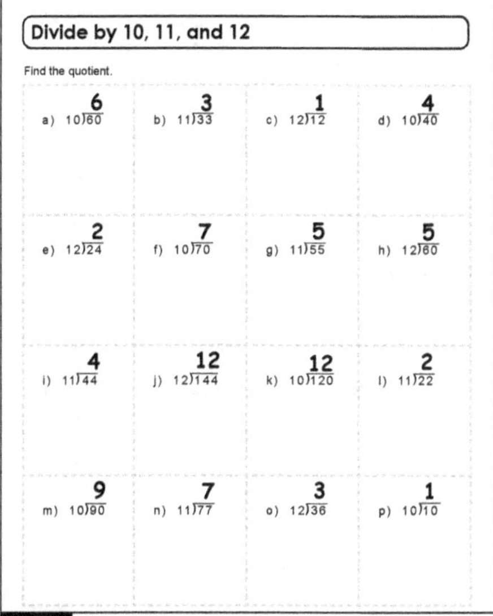

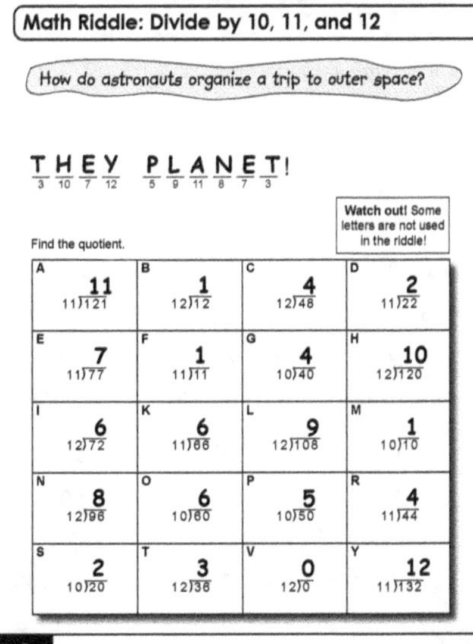

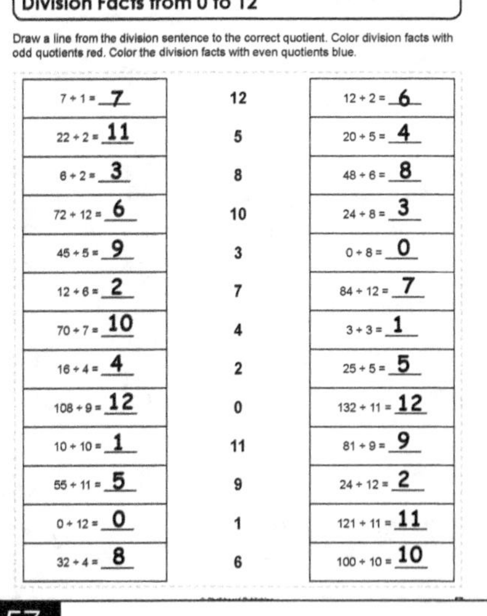

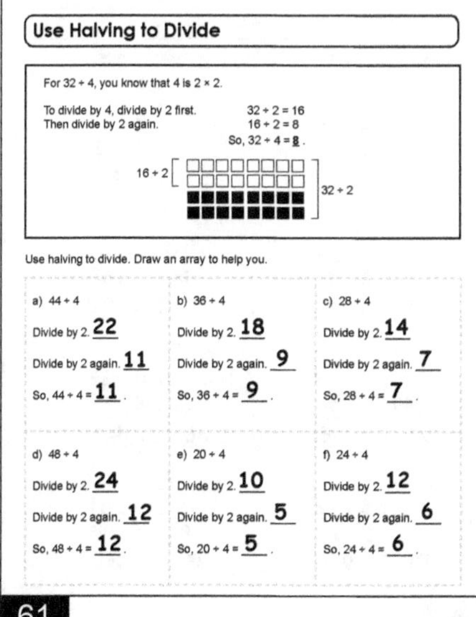

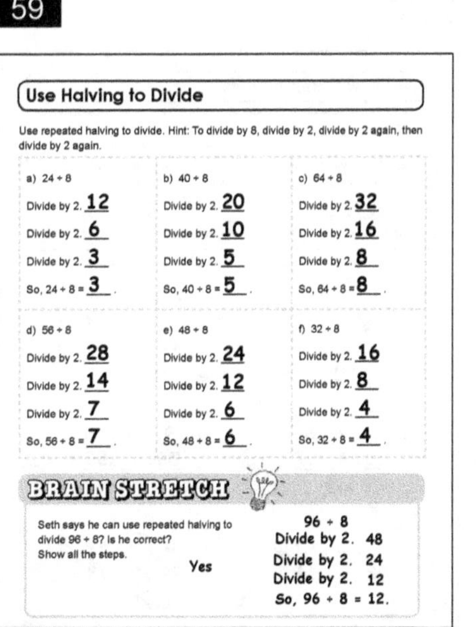

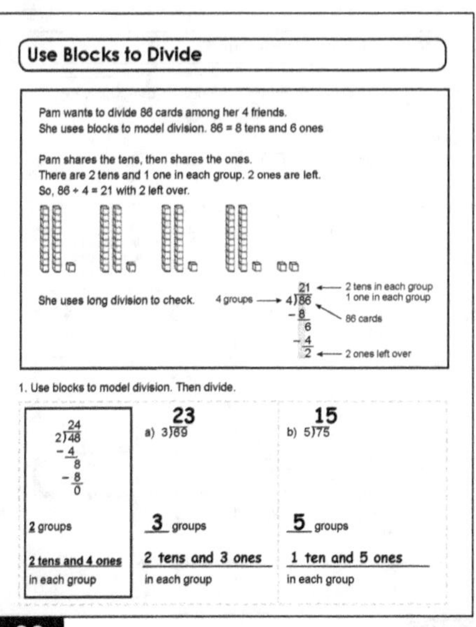

© Chalkboard Publishing

Use Blocks to Divide

Divide. Write how many are left over.

a) 5)67 → **13**
  5 groups
  13 in each group
  2 left over

b) 4)89 → **22**
  4 groups
  22 in each group
  1 left over

c) 3)92 → **30**
  3 groups
  30 in each group
  2 left over

d) 2)45 → **22**
  2 groups
  22 in each group
  1 left over

e) 4)78 → **19**
  4 groups
  19 in each group
  2 left over

f) 6)39 → **6**
  6 groups
  6 in each group
  3 left over

Jenny plants 88 trees in 4 rows. How many trees are in each row? Use a model to help you solve the problem.

88 ÷ 4 = **22**

`64`

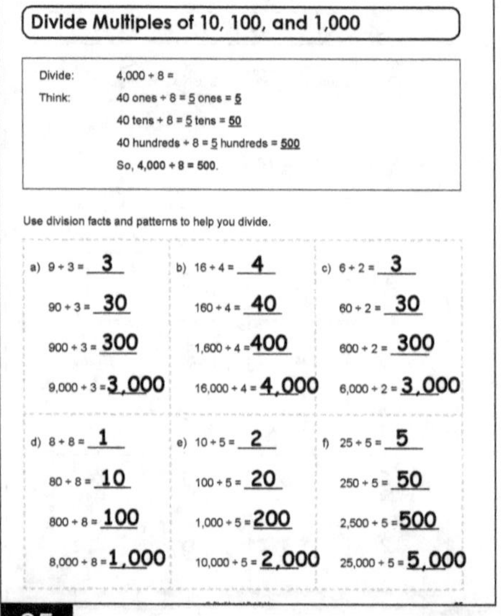

Divide Multiples of 10, 100, and 1,000

Divide: 4,000 ÷ 8 =

Think:
40 ones ÷ 8 = **5** ones = **5**
40 tens ÷ 8 = **5** tens = **50**
40 hundreds ÷ 8 = **5** hundreds = **500**
So, 4,000 ÷ 8 = 500.

Use division facts and patterns to help you divide.

a) 9 ÷ 3 = **3**
90 ÷ 3 = **30**
900 ÷ 3 = **300**
9,000 ÷ 3 = **3,000**

b) 16 ÷ 4 = **4**
160 ÷ 4 = **40**
1,600 ÷ 4 = **400**
16,000 ÷ 4 = **4,000**

c) 6 ÷ 2 = **3**
60 ÷ 2 = **30**
600 ÷ 2 = **300**
6,000 ÷ 2 = **3,000**

d) 8 ÷ 8 = **1**
80 ÷ 8 = **10**
800 ÷ 8 = **100**
8,000 ÷ 8 = **1,000**

e) 10 ÷ 5 = **2**
100 ÷ 5 = **20**
1,000 ÷ 5 = **200**
10,000 ÷ 5 = **2,000**

f) 25 ÷ 5 = **5**
250 ÷ 5 = **50**
2,500 ÷ 5 = **500**
25,000 ÷ 5 = **5,000**

`65`

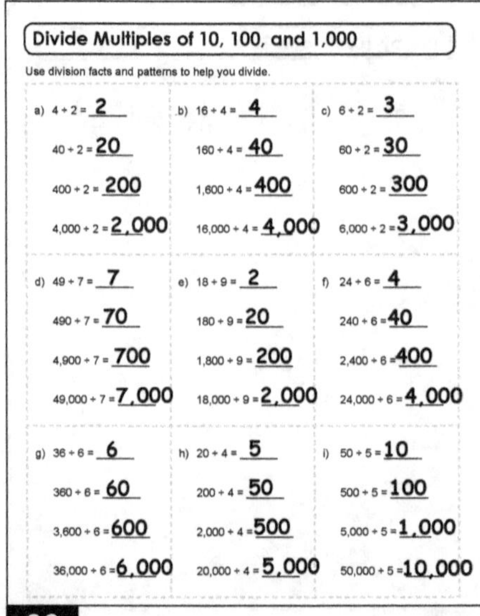

Divide Multiples of 10, 100, and 1,000

Use division facts and patterns to help you divide.

a) 4 ÷ 2 = **2**
40 ÷ 2 = **20**
400 ÷ 2 = **200**
4,000 ÷ 2 = **2,000**

b) 16 ÷ 4 = **4**
160 ÷ 4 = **40**
1,600 ÷ 4 = **400**
16,000 ÷ 4 = **4,000**

c) 6 ÷ 2 = **3**
60 ÷ 2 = **30**
600 ÷ 2 = **300**
6,000 ÷ 2 = **3,000**

d) 49 ÷ 7 = **7**
490 ÷ 7 = **70**
4,900 ÷ 7 = **700**
49,000 ÷ 7 = **7,000**

e) 18 ÷ 9 = **2**
180 ÷ 9 = **20**
1,800 ÷ 9 = **200**
18,000 ÷ 9 = **2,000**

f) 24 ÷ 6 = **4**
240 ÷ 6 = **40**
2,400 ÷ 6 = **400**
24,000 ÷ 6 = **4,000**

g) 36 ÷ 6 = **6**
360 ÷ 6 = **60**
3,600 ÷ 6 = **600**
36,000 ÷ 6 = **6,000**

h) 20 ÷ 4 = **5**
200 ÷ 4 = **50**
2,000 ÷ 4 = **500**
20,000 ÷ 4 = **5,000**

i) 50 ÷ 5 = **10**
500 ÷ 5 = **100**
5,000 ÷ 5 = **1,000**
50,000 ÷ 5 = **10,000**

`66`

Divide Multiples of 10, 100, and 1,000

Use division facts and patterns to help you divide.

a) 48 ÷ 12 = **4**
480 ÷ 12 = **40**
4,800 ÷ 12 = **400**
48,000 ÷ 12 = **4,000**

b) 54 ÷ 9 = **6**
540 ÷ 9 = **60**
5,400 ÷ 9 = **600**
54,000 ÷ 9 = **6,000**

c) 32 ÷ 8 = **4**
320 ÷ 8 = **40**
3,200 ÷ 8 = **400**
32,000 ÷ 8 = **4,000**

Divide.

70 ÷ 7 = **10**
2,400 ÷ 6 = **400**
3,000 ÷ 3 = **1,000**
80 ÷ 2 = **40**
6,300 ÷ 7 = **900**
7,000 ÷ 7 = **1,000**
200 ÷ 2 = **100**

6,400 ÷ 8 = **800**
20 ÷ 4 = **5**
200 ÷ 4 = **50**
4,800 ÷ 4 = **1,200**
60 ÷ 3 = **20**
720 ÷ 9 = **80**
140 ÷ 7 = **20**

5,600 ÷ 8 = **700**
8,100 ÷ 9 = **900**
50 ÷ 10 = **5**
350 ÷ 7 = **50**
5,000 ÷ 5 = **1,000**
120 ÷ 3 = **40**
6,000 ÷ 3 = **2,000**

`67`

Math Riddle: Divide Multiples of 10, 100, and 1,000

How did the rabbit try to make gold soup?

HE USED TWENTY-FOUR
900 400 60 30 400 800 1,200 90 400 1,000 1,200 20 500 40 60 50

CARROTS!
700 10 50 50 40 1,200 30

Watch out! Some letters are not used in the riddle!

Find the quotient.

A 7)70 = **10**	**C** 8)5600 = **700**	**D** 8)6400 = **800**	**E** 6)2400 = **400**	
F 4)2000 = **500**	**G** 7)700 = **100**	**H** 9)8100 = **900**	**I** 9)720 = **80**	
M 3)240 = **80**	**N** 3)3000 = **1000**	**O** 4)160 = **40**	**R** 10)500 = **50**	
S 2)60 = **30**	**T** 4)4800 = **1200**	**U** 7)420 = **60**	**W** 7)630 = **90**	
Y 3)60 = **20**	**Z** 5)500 = **100**			

`68`

Math Riddle: Division Fun

I am a wind-up toy that can walk. I am made from tinplate and stand just 6 inches tall, who am I?

I AM THE FIRST ROBOT
10 11 12 5 4 7 2 10 9 400 5 9 6 60 6 5

TOY, LILLIPUT!
5 6 20 70 10 70 70 10 8 3 5

Watch out! Some letters are not used in the riddle!

Find the quotient.

A 7)77 = **11**	**B** 100)6000 = **60**	**C** 3)45 = **15**	**D** 2)64 = **32**	
E 9)63 = **7**	**F** 9)18 = **2**	**G** 40)600 = **15**	**H** 2)8 = **4**	
I 12)120 = **10**	**J** 10)140 = **14**	**K** 100)5000 = **50**	**L** 10)700 = **70**	
M 5)60 = **12**	**O** 6)36 = **6**	**P** 10)80 = **8**	**R** 5)45 = **9**	
S 10)4000 = **400**	**T** 4)20 = **5**	**U** 7)21 = **3**	**Y** 10)200 = **20**	

`69`

Math Riddle: Division Fun

I attempt to create computer programs that think for themselves, like human brains. What am I?

I AM ARTIFICIAL
1 12 8 12 4 7 1 9 1 5 1 12 10

INTELLIGENCE!
1 6 7 2 10 10 1 3 2 6 5 2

Watch out! Some letters are not used in the riddle!

Find the quotient.

A 2)24 = **12**	**B** 2)22 = **11**	**C** 12)60 = **5**	**D** 10)140 = **14**
E 3)6 = **2**	**F** 8)72 = **9**	**G** 8)24 = **3**	**H** 100)1500 = **15**
I 4)4 = **1**	**L** 10)100 = **10**	**M** 2)16 = **8**	**N** 1)6 = **6**
O 9)99 = **11**	**R** 7)28 = **4**	**T** 7)49 = **7**	

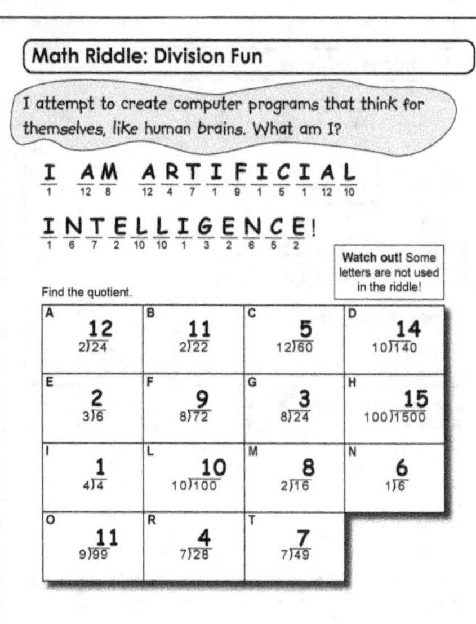

`70`

Division with Remainders

Use multiplication and addition to find an answer with a remainder.

To find 22 ÷ 3, think of a factor of 3 that is close to 22.
Think: 7 × 3 = **21**
So you know there are 3 groups of 7 in 22.

But how do you get 22? Count up from 21 to find the remainder.
21 + **1** = 22, so the remainder is 1.
So, 22 ÷ 3 = **7 Remainder 1, or 7 R 1**.

Solve. Use multiplication and addition to find an answer with a remainder.

a) 19 ÷ 2 =
Think: 9 × **2** = 18
18 + **1** = **19**
So, 19 ÷ 2 = **9R1**

b) 13 ÷ 2 =
Think: **6** × **2** = **12**
12 + **1** = **13**
So, 13 ÷ 2 = **6R1**

c) 67 ÷ 7 =
Think: **9** × **7** = 63
63 + **4** = **67**
So, 67 ÷ 7 = **9R4**

d) 55 ÷ 6 =
Think: **9** × **6** = **54**
54 + **1** = **55**
So, 55 ÷ 6 = **9R1**

e) 44 ÷ 6 =
Think: **7** × **6** = 42
42 + **2** = **44**
So, 44 ÷ 6 = **7R2**

f) 73 ÷ 8 =
Think: **9** × **8** = 72
72 + **1** = **73**
So, 73 ÷ 8 = **9R1**

`71`

Division with Remainders

Solve. Use multiplication and addition to find an answer with a remainder.

a) 15 ÷ 2 =
Think: **7** × 2 = **14**
14 + **1** = **15**
So, 15 ÷ 2 = **7R1**

b) 25 ÷ 2 =
Think: **12** × 2 = **24**
24 + **1** = **25**
So, 25 ÷ 2 = **12R1**

c) 47 ÷ 7 =
Think: **6** × 7 = **42**
42 + **5** = **47**
So, 47 ÷ 7 = **6R5**

d) 63 ÷ 6 =
Think: **10** × 6 = **60**
60 + **3** = **63**
So, 63 ÷ 6 = **10R3**

e) 54 ÷ 7 =
Think: **7** × 7 = **49**
49 + **5** = **54**
So, 54 ÷ 7 = **7R5**

f) 36 ÷ 8 =
Think: **4** × 8 = **32**
32 + **4** = **36**
So, 36 ÷ 8 = **4R4**

g) 78 ÷ 8 =
Think: **9** × 8 = **72**
72 + **6** = **78**
So, 78 ÷ 8 = **9R6**

h) 85 ÷ 9 =
Think: **9** × 9 = **81**
81 + **4** = **85**
So, 85 ÷ 9 = **9R4**

`72`

Page 73 — Division with Remainders

Solve. Use multiplication and addition to find an answer with a remainder.

a) $37 \div 5 =$ _____
Think: $7 \times 5 = 35$
$35 + 2 = 37$
So, $37 \div 5 = $ **7R2**.

b) $29 \div 4 =$ _____
Think: $7 \times 4 = 28$
$28 + 1 = 29$
So, $29 \div 4 = $ **7R1**.

c) $89 \div 7 =$ _____
Think: $12 \times 7 = 84$
$84 + 5 = 89$
So, $89 \div 7 = $ **12R5**.

d) $57 \div 6 =$ _____
Think: $9 \times 6 = 54$
$54 + 3 = 57$
So, $57 \div 6 = $ **9R3**.

e) $25 \div 3 =$ _____
Think: $8 \times 3 = 24$
$24 + 1 = 25$
So, $25 \div 3 = $ **8R1**.

f) $44 \div 8 =$ _____
Think: $5 \times 8 = 40$
$40 + 4 = 44$
So, $44 \div 8 = $ **5R4**.

g) $63 \div 5 =$ _____
Think: $12 \times 5 = 60$
$60 + 3 = 63$
So, $63 \div 5 = $ **12R3**.

h) $57 \div 9 =$ _____
Think: $6 \times 9 = 54$
$54 + 3 = 57$
So, $57 \div 9 = $ **6R3**.

Page 74 — Divide a Two-Digit Number by a One-Digit Number

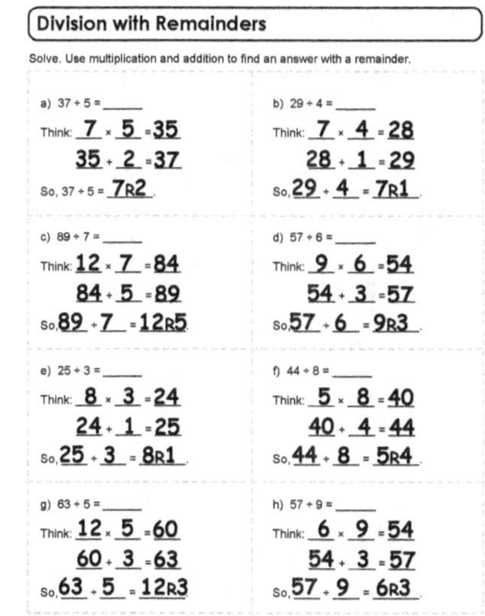

Step 1: Divide to find how many tens can go in each group.

2 tens in each group → 2
2 groups → 2⟌51

Step 2: Multiply: 4 tens are placed. Subtract: 1 ten is left. So, 1 ten and 1 one are left. Write 1 beside the 1 ten.

Step 3: Divide to find how many ones can go in each group.

25 ← 5 ones in each group

Step 4: Multiply 10 ones are placed. Subtract to find that 1 one is left. So, the answer is 25 R 1.

R means remainder.

Find the quotient. Hint: The answer in division is called the **quotient**.

a) **8R1** 8⟌65
b) **1R3** 7⟌10
c) **9R2** 5⟌47
d) **22** 3⟌66

e) **9R4** 7⟌67
f) **38R1** 2⟌77
g) **4R2** 4⟌18
h) **5R2** 5⟌27

Page 75 — Divide a Two-Digit Number by a One-Digit Number

Divide. Hint: As you work, line up the tens and ones. Shade the tens column orange. Shade the ones column yellow.

a) **11** 7⟌77
b) **14** 7⟌98
c) **30R1** 2⟌61
d) **4R1** 3⟌13

e) **8R2** 3⟌26
f) **25** 2⟌50
g) **25** 3⟌75
h) **19R1** 2⟌39

i) **21** 4⟌84
j) **6R1** 3⟌19
k) **18** 5⟌90
l) **7R4** 7⟌53

Page 76 — Divide a Two-Digit Number by a One-Digit Number

Divide. Hint: As you work, line up the tens and ones. Shade the tens column orange. Shade the ones column yellow.

a) **6R2** 7⟌44
b) **43** 2⟌86
c) **7R4** 5⟌39
d) **20R1** 2⟌41

e) **18** 3⟌54
f) **15R1** 6⟌91
g) **16R1** 4⟌65
h) **28R1** 2⟌57

i) **24R1** 2⟌49
j) **4R1** 6⟌25
k) **12R6** 7⟌90
l) **29** 3⟌87

Page 77 — Divide a Two-Digit Number by a One-Digit Number

Divide. Hint: As you work, line up the tens and ones. Shade the tens column orange. Shade the ones column yellow.

a) **9R7** 8⟌79
b) **16** 3⟌48
c) **42R1** 2⟌85
d) **32** 2⟌64

e) **22R2** 3⟌68
f) **5R4** 7⟌39
g) **7R4** 6⟌46
h) **12** 8⟌96

i) **13R4** 5⟌69
j) **8R5** 9⟌77
k) **13** 5⟌65
l) **14R1** 4⟌57

Page 78 — Divide Multi-Digit Numbers

Divide.

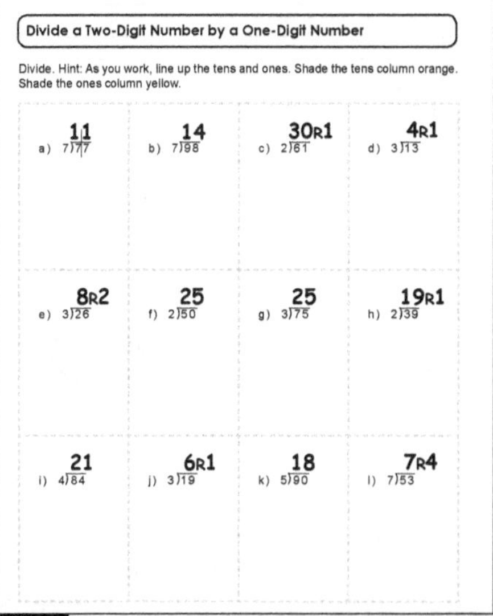

$$\begin{array}{r} 78 \\ 4\,\overline{)312} \\ -28 \\ \hline 32 \\ -32 \\ \hline 0 \end{array}$$

Hint: There are fewer hundreds than groups. So, the division starts with the tens.

a) **495R1** 2⟌991
b) **172R1** 2⟌345

c) **67** 9⟌603
d) **34** 7⟌238
e) **61** 6⟌366
f) **111R2** 8⟌890

g) **131R4** 5⟌659
h) **134R1** 4⟌537
i) **84R2** 3⟌254
j) **62R1** 3⟌187

Page 79 — Divide Multi-Digit Numbers

Divide. Hint: As you work, line up the hundreds, tens, and ones. Shade the tens column orange. Shade the ones column yellow. Shade the hundreds column green.

a) **131R3** 4⟌527
b) **58R3** 5⟌293
c) **124R5** 6⟌749
d) **34R2** 8⟌274

e) **314R1** 3⟌943
f) **52R3** 9⟌471
g) **127** 6⟌762
h) **28R2** 5⟌142

i) **218R2** 3⟌656
j) **215R1** 2⟌431
k) **412R1** 2⟌825
l) **122** 4⟌488

Page 80 — Divide Multi-Digit Numbers

Divide. Hint: As you work, line up the hundreds, tens, and ones. Shade the tens column orange. Shade the ones column yellow. Shade the hundreds column green.

a) **152** 5⟌760
b) **37** 7⟌259
c) **187R1** 4⟌749
d) **46** 8⟌368

e) **217R1** 3⟌652
f) **41** 9⟌369
g) **74** 6⟌444
h) **151** 5⟌755

i) **91** 7⟌637
j) **428R1** 2⟌857
k) **55R1** 2⟌111
l) **162R2** 3⟌488

Page 81 — Estimate a Quotient

Use **compatible numbers** to estimate a quotient. Compatible numbers are numbers that divide evenly.

Estimate: $243 \div 6$. Divide 6 into the first 2 digits. How many 6s are in 24?

Think: $24 \div 6 = 4$
$240 \div 6 = 40$ Since it is an estimate, write 0 for the ones digit.
The estimated quotient is 40.

Use compatible numbers to estimate the quotient. Show your work.

a) 5⟌355
$35 \div 5 = 7$
$350 \div 5 = 70$

b) 3⟌246
$24 \div 3 = 8$
$240 \div 3 = 80$

c) 4⟌284
$28 \div 4 = 7$
$280 \div 4 = 70$

d) 2⟌128
$12 \div 2 = 6$
$120 \div 2 = 60$

e) 6⟌468
$42 \div 6 = 7$
$420 \div 6 = 70$

f) 7⟌581
$56 \div 7 = 8$
$560 \div 7 = 80$

Estimate a Quotient

Estimate: 312 ÷ 4
Think: What multiples of 4 are close to 31?

28 is too low   32 is close to 31   36 is too high

32 ÷ 4 = 8   So, try 8.
320 ÷ 4 = 80   Write 0 for the ones digit.
The estimated quotient is 80.

Estimate the quotient. Show your work.

a) $3\overline{)143}$

$12 \div 3 = 4$
$120 \div 3 = 40$

b) $4\overline{)254}$

$24 \div 4 = 6$
$240 \div 4 = 60$

c) $5\overline{)224}$

$20 \div 5 = 4$
$200 \div 5 = 40$

d) $6\overline{)431}$

$42 \div 6 = 7$
$420 \div 6 = 70$

e) $8\overline{)634}$

$64 \div 8 = 8$
$640 \div 8 = 80$

f) $5\overline{)365}$

$35 \div 5 = 7$
$350 \div 5 = 70$

82

Division Fact Fun—Test 1

1.	12 ÷ 12 = 1		21.	0 ÷ 5 = 0
2.	22 ÷ 11 = 2		22.	66 ÷ 6 = 11
3.	90 ÷ 10 = 9		23.	35 ÷ 7 = 5
4.	121 ÷ 11 = 11		24.	48 ÷ 8 = 6
5.	40 ÷ 8 = 5		25.	88 ÷ 8 = 11
6.	7 ÷ 7 = 1		26.	0 ÷ 10 = 0
7.	0 ÷ 6 = 0		27.	77 ÷ 11 = 7
8.	35 ÷ 5 = 7		28.	60 ÷ 12 = 5
9.	44 ÷ 4 = 11		29.	4 ÷ 1 = 4
10.	12 ÷ 3 = 4		30.	108 ÷ 9 = 12
11.	8 ÷ 2 = 4		31.	24 ÷ 2 = 12
12.	3 ÷ 1 = 3		32.	42 ÷ 7 = 6
13.	132 ÷ 12 = 11		33.	15 ÷ 3 = 5
14.	55 ÷ 11 = 5		34.	12 ÷ 6 = 2
15.	120 ÷ 10 = 12		35.	30 ÷ 5 = 6
16.	99 ÷ 9 = 11		36.	8 ÷ 4 = 2
17.	72 ÷ 8 = 9		37.	20 ÷ 10 = 2
18.	6 ÷ 6 = 1		38.	96 ÷ 12 = 8
19.	20 ÷ 5 = 4		39.	33 ÷ 3 = 11
20.	48 ÷ 4 = 12		40.	16 ÷ 2 = 8

Number Correct /40

83

Division Fact Fun—Test 2

1.	6 ÷ 2 = 3		21.	60 ÷ 10 = 6
2.	0 ÷ 3 = 0		22.	42 ÷ 6 = 7
3.	28 ÷ 4 = 7		23.	70 ÷ 7 = 10
4.	50 ÷ 5 = 10		24.	45 ÷ 9 = 5
5.	72 ÷ 6 = 12		25.	14 ÷ 2 = 7
6.	0 ÷ 7 = 0		26.	5 ÷ 1 = 5
7.	16 ÷ 8 = 2		27.	108 ÷ 12 = 9
8.	54 ÷ 9 = 6		28.	33 ÷ 11 = 3
9.	80 ÷ 10 = 8		29.	18 ÷ 9 = 2
10.	88 ÷ 11 = 8		30.	32 ÷ 8 = 4
11.	120 ÷ 12 = 10		31.	77 ÷ 7 = 11
12.	9 ÷ 1 = 9		32.	30 ÷ 6 = 5
13.	3 ÷ 3 = 1		33.	5 ÷ 5 = 1
14.	55 ÷ 5 = 11		34.	36 ÷ 4 = 9
15.	63 ÷ 7 = 9		35.	6 ÷ 3 = 2
16.	27 ÷ 9 = 3		36.	10 ÷ 2 = 5
17.	66 ÷ 11 = 6		37.	0 ÷ 1 = 0
18.	12 ÷ 2 = 6		38.	72 ÷ 12 = 6
19.	24 ÷ 4 = 6		39.	40 ÷ 10 = 4
20.	48 ÷ 6 = 8		40.	0 ÷ 8 = 0

Number Correct /40

84

Division Fact Fun—Test 3

1.	12 ÷ 1 = 12		21.	2 ÷ 2 = 1
2.	22 ÷ 2 = 11		22.	36 ÷ 4 = 9
3.	9 ÷ 3 = 3		23.	18 ÷ 6 = 3
4.	16 ÷ 4 = 4		24.	24 ÷ 8 = 3
5.	40 ÷ 5 = 8		25.	100 ÷ 10 = 10
6.	54 ÷ 6 = 9		26.	84 ÷ 12 = 7
7.	14 ÷ 7 = 2		27.	27 ÷ 3 = 9
8.	64 ÷ 8 = 8		28.	15 ÷ 5 = 3
9.	72 ÷ 9 = 8		29.	49 ÷ 7 = 7
10.	10 ÷ 10 = 1		30.	81 ÷ 9 = 9
11.	110 ÷ 11 = 10		31.	1 ÷ 1 = 1
12.	36 ÷ 12 = 3		32.	44 ÷ 11 = 4
13.	25 ÷ 5 = 5		33.	0 ÷ 4 = 0
14.	60 ÷ 6 = 10		34.	36 ÷ 3 = 12
15.	28 ÷ 7 = 4		35.	20 ÷ 2 = 10
16.	88 ÷ 8 = 11		36.	6 ÷ 1 = 6
17.	9 ÷ 9 = 1		37.	36 ÷ 6 = 6
18.	30 ÷ 10 = 3		38.	55 ÷ 5 = 11
19.	0 ÷ 11 = 0		39.	4 ÷ 4 = 1
20.	144 ÷ 12 = 12		40.	18 ÷ 3 = 6

Number Correct /40

85

Division Fact Fun—Test 4

1.	7 ÷ 1 = 7		21.	20 ÷ 5 = 4
2.	20 ÷ 2 = 10		22.	16 ÷ 4 = 4
3.	6 ÷ 3 = 2		23.	42 ÷ 6 = 7
4.	20 ÷ 4 = 5		24.	32 ÷ 8 = 4
5.	35 ÷ 5 = 7		25.	10 ÷ 5 = 2
6.	48 ÷ 6 = 8		26.	108 ÷ 12 = 9
7.	77 ÷ 7 = 11		27.	21 ÷ 3 = 7
8.	80 ÷ 8 = 10		28.	10 ÷ 5 = 2
9.	108 ÷ 9 = 12		29.	49 ÷ 7 = 7
10.	100 ÷ 10 = 10		30.	9 ÷ 9 = 1
11.	22 ÷ 11 = 2		31.	0 ÷ 1 = 0
12.	144 ÷ 12 = 12		32.	99 ÷ 11 = 9
13.	55 ÷ 5 = 11		33.	32 ÷ 4 = 8
14.	18 ÷ 6 = 3		34.	36 ÷ 3 = 12
15.	42 ÷ 7 = 6		35.	22 ÷ 2 = 11
16.	64 ÷ 8 = 8		36.	2 ÷ 1 = 2
17.	81 ÷ 9 = 9		37.	36 ÷ 6 = 6
18.	30 ÷ 10 = 3		38.	25 ÷ 5 = 5
19.	0 ÷ 11 = 0		39.	40 ÷ 4 = 10
20.	36 ÷ 12 = 3		40.	15 ÷ 3 = 5

Number Correct /40

86

Division Fact Fun—Test 5

1.	12 ÷ 12 = 1		21.	0 ÷ 5 = 0
2.	22 ÷ 11 = 2		22.	66 ÷ 6 = 11
3.	90 ÷ 10 = 9		23.	45 ÷ 9 = 5
4.	121 ÷ 11 = 11		24.	48 ÷ 8 = 6
5.	40 ÷ 8 = 5		25.	88 ÷ 8 = 11
6.	7 ÷ 7 = 1		26.	0 ÷ 10 = 0
7.	0 ÷ 6 = 0		27.	77 ÷ 11 = 7
8.	35 ÷ 5 = 7		28.	60 ÷ 12 = 5
9.	44 ÷ 4 = 11		29.	4 ÷ 1 = 4
10.	12 ÷ 3 = 4		30.	108 ÷ 9 = 12
11.	8 ÷ 2 = 4		31.	24 ÷ 2 = 12
12.	3 ÷ 1 = 3		32.	42 ÷ 7 = 6
13.	132 ÷ 12 = 11		33.	15 ÷ 3 = 5
14.	55 ÷ 11 = 5		34.	12 ÷ 6 = 2
15.	120 ÷ 10 = 12		35.	30 ÷ 5 = 6
16.	99 ÷ 9 = 11		36.	8 ÷ 4 = 2
17.	72 ÷ 8 = 9		37.	20 ÷ 10 = 2
18.	6 ÷ 6 = 1		38.	96 ÷ 12 = 8
19.	20 ÷ 5 = 4		39.	33 ÷ 3 = 11
20.	48 ÷ 4 = 12		40.	16 ÷ 2 = 8

Number Correct /40

87

Division Fact Fun—Test 6

1.	80 ÷ 4 = 20		21.	100 ÷ 5 = 20
2.	180 ÷ 2 = 90		22.	1,200 ÷ 4 = 300
3.	3,000 ÷ 6 = 500		23.	48,000 ÷ 6 = 8,000
4.	40 ÷ 4 = 10		24.	5,600 ÷ 8 = 700
5.	6,000 ÷ 5 = 1,200		25.	90 ÷ 10 = 9
6.	240 ÷ 6 = 40		26.	1,200 ÷ 12 = 100
7.	5,600 ÷ 7 = 800		27.	90 ÷ 3 = 30
8.	960 ÷ 8 = 120		28.	2,500 ÷ 5 = 500
9.	70,000 ÷ 10 = 7,000		29.	350 ÷ 7 = 50
10.	1,100 ÷ 10 = 110		30.	99,000 ÷ 9 = 11,000
11.	11,000 ÷ 11 = 1,000		31.	48,000 ÷ 4 = 12,000
12.	7,200 ÷ 12 = 600		32.	880 ÷ 11 = 80
13.	450 ÷ 5 = 90		33.	2,400 ÷ 4 = 600
14.	6,600 ÷ 6 = 1,100		34.	600 ÷ 3 = 200
15.	840 ÷ 7 = 120		35.	1,400 ÷ 2 = 700
16.	80 ÷ 8 = 10		36.	250 ÷ 5 = 50
17.	63,000 ÷ 9 = 7,000		37.	36,000 ÷ 6 = 6,000
18.	5,000 ÷ 10 = 500		38.	60 ÷ 5 = 12
19.	990 ÷ 11 = 90		39.	30 ÷ 5 = 6
20.	480 ÷ 12 = 40		40.	150 ÷ 3 = 50

Number Correct /40

88